MW00647672

DEDICATION

I want to thank and dedicate this book to my husband, Joe. Your love, persistence, and devotion to me and our family made our journey possible. You trusted, when I was weak in faith, that our steps would be ordered by God. You have been committed to me and our family from day one, even when I was scared, unsteady, and not sure what my next steps should be.

To our awesome children we have been blessed to raise, you are more than I could have ever imagined when I prayed for God to bless me with children. Parenting was the hardest job ever, but the most rewarding. A lot of my life lessons have come from learning to be a parent to you. Jonathan, Jared, Chris, Lori, Zach, and Alijah – I love you all and am so very thankful you were given to me to be your mother.

To my grandchildren, you are just that – "Grand" – and your Maw-Maw is so thankful for you. I hope you always remember that with God, all things are possible.

GRAB YOUR FREE GIFT!

(RETAILS FOR $19.99...Yours FREE!)

Do you want to get your blended family in harmony? Do you want peace of mind?

You should download the workbook for this edition right now. It can help implement the concepts and help you move forward in your blended family to achieving the life you want.

To access your gift:

1. Go to HelpFamiliesThrive.com/gift.
2. Tell us where to email the access link.
3. Check your email, then download the PDF.
4. Use it alongside reading the book.
5. You and your family dynamic are in for a harmonious shift!

PRAISE FOR
"LIFE IN THE BLENDER"

"May Simpson's new book, "Life in the Blender," is a must read for anyone who is part of a blended family! She has a huge heart, and her sincere approach to this critical topic is outstanding. This book is filled with valuable takeaways for anyone facing the challenge of family stress!"

—Don Hutson, #1 NY Times & Wall Street Journal
Best Selling Author and Hall of Fame Speaker

I had the honor of working with May and I got to see first-hand how she navigated a blended family. I learned even more when I read her book. She gives very practical examples of what worked for her family and what didn't. If you are in a blended family, I would highly recommend that you and your spouse take the time to read what May shares. There are so many nuggets inside the book that are very beneficial for families that are blended, and it will even benefit those that aren't. Take the time to not only read it, but also implement the action steps she shares with you. I truly believe that if you do, your family will grow closer.

—Ronda DeLaughter
Illuminates Hope
Personal Empowerment Coach

Some people say you can't judge a book by its cover. This book is the exception! May Simpson covers this book with her own life experiences, being very candid, honest, and transparent. This is not a textbook, but is written in a down-home, earthy, easy to read style. If you are willing to work these principles, not with selfish motives, then she can teach you how to be successful. You will be free to make the right choices and stay clear of peer pressure by choosing the right friends. The most important principle is putting Jesus in the center of every detail of your life.

Some of the most successful people in life understand this important principle: It's not how you start or where you come from that is important, but where you are going and how it ends that counts. Paul writes in Philippians 3:13 (Worldwide English Bible), "My brothers, I do not yet think that I have got all the things of Christ. But there is one thing that I am doing. I forget what is behind me and reach out to what is ahead of me."

This is the essence of what May Simpson will train you to do and be. Let her experiences and her faith guide you. With this program you can't help but succeed!

—Elizabeth Smithers
Associate Pastor, Faith Victory Church
Frankfort, Ky

"The steps of a good man are ordered by the Lord: and He delighteth in his way."

— **Psalms 37:23**

CONTENTS

FOREWORD

Many people have asked me how I became a successful entrepreneur, currently owning five pool and spa stores along with a motel near Kentucky Lake. I tell them I was blessed with a dad who had a great vision, and he passed it on to me and my three siblings. All four of his children work in the pool industry.

He taught us we are all children who must learn as we grow, step by step: from crawling to falling, to failing in business, as we all have become aware of; to stepping into the plans for our lives.

He taught us to stand upon knowing that our children would fall; that they, too, would have to learn the steps, as we all do. He also knew that his children would always be his children, even when they lost their way.

My wife, Cindi, and I both agree one of the hardest lessons learned throughout our life's journey has been the steps to blending our families together after we both had experienced going through divorce.

When love is found the second time around, it often comes with extra gifts in the form of children. With time, love, patience, and empathy, those two families can become one. One family, who loves posing for silly pictures in swimming pools. One family, who can't spend eight hours in the car without having a "pull the car over" episode – even when the kids are all in their 20s. You are still learning the steps to manage them. One family, who mourn together over the loss of grandparents. One family. Just like a traditional, non-blended family, you are forever learning steps along the journey. You have increasing challenges, your patience is tried, occasional tears, and ultimately, a sense of peace.

We certainly don't want any of our children ever to go through the loss of a spouse or through a divorce. But if that ever happens, we know that we have trained them to focus on their faith, to take the necessary steps to overcome, and not to focus on their own feelings of anger, loss, disappointment, or abandonment. We believed the scripture, "Train up a child in the way he should go and when he is old, he will not depart from it" (Prov. 22:6).

I would like to have had this book as a reference for Cindi and me when we merged our families. It would have helped us to navigate our lives with more ease. We share our story in this book about how we had challenges; however, we knew we were going to make it work. We were committed to each other and to the children. We believed our steps would be made clear for us and the path would be shown to us. The path and each step were shown, and we succeeded.

May Simpson worked for us for a few years as our service manager. We grew to love her and her family. Their journey was like ours; no instructions and no manual came with managing life, especially a blended family mix.

May has done an outstanding job of showing how to navigate and make life work, not only in a blended family, as we had to learn. The way she explains the steps that helped her all along her life's journey can also help you to step into your greatest life ever.

I encourage you to read this book, do the action steps, use it as a guide for you to keep stepping into the life God intended for you to have. This book is full of tools to use and to place into your tool belt. Our goal should be to fully enjoy the life we have here and to raise healthy, successful children. Then, when our earthly journey here ends, to know we did everything our Creator had for us to do and accomplish.

Our children are our next generation, and when you learn to thrive, your children will learn that as well. The heritage you want to leave will continue through them. Thankfully, Cindi and I both learned that from our parents.

Brad Cook,
Owner of Aloha Pools and Spas

PREFACE

"The journey of a thousand miles begins with one step."
— **Lao Tzu**

I was recently at a conference in Nashville, Tennessee, where the emcee asked me to come on stage and dance. This would not only get the energy on stage flowing but would also get the energy flowing in the room. The goal was to help participants be open to receive the messages they were going to hear. My immediate response was, "No! I don't know the steps!" It was the same old message I had told myself for years.

Time and again, I felt as though I couldn't do something the right way, because I just *didn't know how.*

When I got home from the conference it hit me. *Everything in life begins with a step.* Everything we do is one step at a time: dancing, learning a new skill, following a recipe.

I wish I had known the steps, or the recipe, when I first met with the challenges of life as the mother in a blended family. In a time when it felt like everything was spinning around, I was without guidance or instruction.

I believe this book was placed upon my heart to provide just that: the steps, the recipe, for those who need it, especially those hurting from a devastating divorce and trying to create harmony in a blended family.

It is for parents who seek guidance and proven strategies for their family in the areas of family rules and mindset, so they are equipped to create richer experiences in their lives and in the lives of their children.

As the mother in a blended family, I frequently felt like I couldn't do anything right and that I would never succeed because I wasn't "good enough." Joe had two biological children (a boy and a girl) when we married, I had two biological boys, and we adopted two grandsons. I lived it. I felt it. Yet, somehow, I found it in me to take the steps and help my family do the same.

This book is my journey of overcoming – from trying just to survive "the blend" to thriving in it. I persevered through countless trials and failures, and now, with five grown children and a well-adjusted teenager, I think I've got the recipe just right.

I truly believe that *anyone* who is equipped with the right guide can create harmony in a blended family. It is my hope that this book is that guide for you. It doesn't matter where you're starting from. You can be a successful parent with well-adjusted, happy children.

INTRODUCTION

My life story is certainly far from glamorous.

I grew up in Tennessee with parents who were sharecroppers, which is a fancy word for cotton pickers. I was taught sound life principles. Be a kind person, do good to others, treat others as you want to be treated, love God, and make your family a priority.

But I was never taught the steps to handle life's struggles, to handle my emotions, or to deal with limiting beliefs. I was not prepared for how to find the answers regarding pain, turmoil, stress, grief, and all the things life hands you. I was not taught lessons on mindset, skillset, strategies, or ways to implement steps that work to get you what you want, need, or desire to be. I was taught to trust, yet I struggled to fully comprehend how to put that into practice.

I stumbled my way through hopelessness, a sense of not belonging, feelings of being shy and powerless and a loner, fear, sadness, and generally being sick and tired. And, eventually, I got sick of being sick and tired of it all.

One thing I did have was faith. I knew there was a Creator Who loved me and could get me answers. He was the One Who brought me true peace in the midst of the storms of my blended family.

I ask that you go into this book knowing that failure is not in the plan for your life. This is about stepping into a successful journey, even if you have a blended family. Failure is not in God's plan for any of His children. His desire is that you thrive in every endeavor in life. Magic can happen, and you can live a life far beyond anything you can think or imagine. You can reach your destination with determination, commitment, persistence, and faith.

I'm thankful that I pursued a relationship with my Creator. Over my lifetime, I experienced more than I could have handled by myself. Coming from a large family of seven siblings and being the baby in the family, I experienced a lot of love from family that many people never experience, but I also experienced a lot of losses that most people never encounter.

My dad had PTSD (Post-traumatic stress disorder) from World War II, and it embedded a deep fear in me. I saw him have raging fits that scared me, and as a child, I did not understand.

When I was six years old, I watched my mother double over in pain as she heard the news that her mother – the only grandmother I ever knew – had passed away. She was crossing the road and was hit by a car; the driver never stopped.

I experienced a total of four miscarriages all while believing I'd have children. That is turmoil that only someone who has suffered from being told they will never be a mother can fully understand.

I experienced an emotional affair while I was seeking connection in the wrong places. I went through a devastating divorce which was the most emotionally heart-wrenching experience of all the things I experienced. A divorce was never in my plans.

I experienced taking care of my mother, who suffered with Lou Gehrig's Disease, until she passed away with me by her side. It is a terrible disease to watch, to see the body deteriorating around a brilliant mind.

My first sibling to pass away was my brother Steve. He had a terrible car crash. His car flipped and he was thrown from the vehicle. It broke his neck, and he died on impact.

I experienced my oldest sister Mary passing from COPD (Chronic Obstructive Pulmonary Disease) that was heart-wrenching to witness. She could not breathe, and it was a relief for her to leave us. She struggled so.

I took care of my oldest brother Harold when he had throat cancer. I went in one morning to wake him up, only to discover he had passed away in his sleep.

My brother Larry passed away from a heart attack. It had snowed and it appeared he had had the heart attack while stepping onto his back porch. After three days of being unable to reach him, since I was out of town for work, I called the local sheriff's department to go to his home. They found him frozen and covered in snow. I had to go and see him that way – another devastating moment etched in my mind.

In May 2021, my sister Barbara passed away from COVID Pneumonia. Seventeen days later, my sister Janice, closest to me in age, was killed in a car wreck. A lady ran a stop sign at an intersection. My sister never knew what hit her. All my life she had been my best friend. It was yet another tragic loss.

I have just one sibling left. "Unreal" is an understatement.

My father-in-law, who lived with Joe and me for more than three years, had prostate cancer. We were his primary care givers. He moved in at 83 years old and passed at 86. He was a delight to be around. I felt it was a second chance to feel a father's love and to have a dad to love in return. He was full of joy and life, all while suffering pain.

In October 2022, I experienced a head injury from falling out of an inversion table onto concrete. I did not realize I was injured. However, six weeks after the blow to the head, I was experiencing stroke symptoms, with the left side of my body completely paralyzed. I went to Vanderbilt Hospital in Nashville, TN, searching for answers, and found out I had ruptured three vessels in my brain, which caused a massive subdural hematoma. On Dec. 14, 2022, I was in surgery for something I never saw coming. It was yet another journey I had never dreamed I would be on. Now I am an advocate for awareness of head injuries.

Why do I share all of this? A few reasons. I want you to understand that even in pain-filled and devastating times, there is hope. There is faith. And there are steps.

This book is my own hands-on experience. I am not seeking sympathy or empathy for my losses. Rather, I am asking you to see my journey more clearly so you can find inspiration and trust that, if these steps have worked for me, they can be effective for you, as well, no matter the current circumstances of your life or the past you have endured.

Through all of this, I worked one step at a time. Was it easy? No! Was it something I had no choice but to do? Absolutely. For my sanity's sake and my family's sake, I managed through it all.

Those in my life that are part of the blend were also required to take steps. For this book, I asked each of my children to be honest and share from their hearts some of the things they have learned along their life's journey up to this point. Numerous others will also share their journeys and the steps they took to carry on in their times of pain in order to get to a life of thriving within their own blend.

If you are struggling in any area of your life, my hope is this book will give you answers to help you walk out your journey. To get you thriving, rather than merely surviving; to enable you to do more than you ever knew possible; to help you live as never before; and to encourage you to take steps you never imagined you could take, so that you can experience a life of true harmony.

Turn the page with an open mind, remembering that life in the blender is dynamic, so we must adjust and keep moving forward, one step at a time.

This book will explain steps you can take when the path you are on is uncertain and the pain is present.

My goal throughout these chapters is to build hope in you. I want you to find relatable circumstances to guide you along your journey. The steps you take depend on you.

It is time to step into a life you love and help your family to thrive.

CHAPTER 1

EMOTIONAL AFFAIR

Early on in my marriage to my first husband, and prior to having children, I felt that I was emotionally starving. I stepped into an emotional affair to get my emotions fed. I yearned to feel like I belonged, like I mattered, and I was searching to fill the void.

Gerald was a truck driver. I was lonely, I was young, and I was sad. I had gone through a second miscarriage, and I was dealing with loss and rejection. I stepped into this emotional relationship blindly because someone would talk to me. Someone was available to me. I would never allow myself to be unfaithful to my husband because of my high morals; however, I let someone in emotionally. Many affairs start just like that, innocently, and the people involved may never understand how it happened.

During this time, I was singing in a gospel group, so I felt that I was pursuing God. However, pursuing God and knowing God in a personal relationship are quite different. It was like the story of Job in the Bible when he was tried and went through terrible times. His friends told him to curse God and die. However, Job stood in his faith. Afterwards, Job said to God, "I have heard of You, but now my eyes see You." Job 42:5-10 tells Job's story. God gave everything he lost back to him; twice as much as he had before.

I, too, knew about God. I sang about God but, just the same, I did not know God in a deep and personal way. I knew enough as far as believing in Him, and I had been baptized. But it was like a friendship, where I would talk to Him occasionally. It was the type of friendship that is nice, but the relationship is very vague, and that friend will never know the real you. You never get authentic with that friend or have an intimate discussion. They are just friends in passing. I had deep emotional sadness, a longing, and I did not know that what I was looking for was God.

I remember one Sunday morning, my sister Ruth saw the look of sadness in my eyes and said, "You look so far away. Can I pray for you?" She had no clue about the turmoil going on inside me, but I will never forget the words she prayed. "God, you know May, you love May, you know where she is, and You know where you are taking her."

At that point, I tuned her out and I started arguing inwardly with God, yes, He knew where I was. I was not only in this emotional affair, but I'd soon be going into an adulterous affair without His intervention. I was tired of feeling lonely and empty, and I needed more.

Something did happen. My pursuit of God began. I would not have my children today, or the life I have lived, if God, who is rich in mercy, had not intervened. I am thankful for that turning point in my life and thankful my sister loved me and was obedient that day.

I grew to be very committed to my Creator. I began to pursue God instead of the emotional affair. I began to read the Bible, and He said there, "If you seek me, you will find me" (Jer. 29:13). So I sought, and I found Him.

I learned I had to let go of what no longer served me. The emotional affair was certainly not serving me, but I found what I was looking for. God was there all the time. I began to learn I could have fulfilling relationships with peace and passion. I found the verse that says Jesus came to give us life and life more abundant. It is a choice.

I was still not where I wanted to be; however, I continued to read and apply principles that worked, such as this one: "Create in me a clean heart, O God; and renew a right spirit within me. Cast me not away from thy presence; and take not thy Holy Spirit from me. Restore unto me the joy of thy salvation; and uphold me with thy free spirit" (Ps. 51:10-12).

The amplified Bible says renew a right and steadfast spirit within me. If you are unhappy, you are probably within yourself, blaming everyone else. Get out of yourself. Figure out the issue and move on. Easier said than done, correct? No, we have a God who loves us. Ask, believe, and receive, and watch what doors open, and what questions are answered and what miracles can come your way.

I finally found God and began a sincere relationship with Him. It freed me from my emotional affair, and I was finally open to receiving the answers I sought. This was my first solid step to achieving the life I desired.

LESSONS AT A GLANCE

- It is important to recognize if you are starving for something. I had that longing for more, to fill the emptiness in me.
- I was looking for my Creator, the only One Who could fill the emptiness. I, therefore, committed myself to my pursuit of Him.
- I dug in and started reading and listening to find the answers I needed.
- By applying those principles, I found what I was looking for.

YOUR NEXT STEPS

1. Think about what it is you are truly looking for. Is it a life of passion or peace? Is it less stress? Are you searching for your purpose? What will fill the void? Keep your goal at the forefront of your mind as you read this book and throughout each day.

2. If it is God you are seeking, know that you can find Him. Know that by seeking, you will find Him. Be willing to seek and be open to receiving.

3. Take an inventory of your commitment to your pursuit. Where are you right now in your pursuit of the life you want? Be honest with yourself and take time to reflect on it.

4. Decide to be a sponge for new knowledge. Recognize that if you are not where you currently want to be, you can get there by being open and learning. There are so many methods of learning. Try some and see what resonates with you. Whether it is through books, podcasts, videos, or in other formats, the answers you seek are out there.

5. Be ready to apply what you learn and remain dedicated, recognizing that growth and change do not happen overnight. Finding answers and taking steps can be an enjoyable process if you allow it to be.

CHAPTER 2

BECOMING A MOTHER

I got married two months before my 18th birthday. He was the love of my life, and I could not wait to spend the rest of my life with him.

Fast forward eight years. By 26 years old, I had survived the emotional affair and had suffered three miscarriages. The doctors told us to stop trying, that we would never be able to have children. Once again, I felt lost, without hope, and confused. I was back in a mental and emotional place I had hoped I would never be in again.

Thankfully, I had already started the journey of learning about our Creator and how much He loved me. I learned that we walk by faith and not by sight. I learned to make my petitions known to God, to ask, believe, and receive. However, I did not know there were steps to the journey of faith.

I wanted a baby so badly and was obsessed with being a mother. One night I was at a baby shower, and my mother-in-law was asked when she was going to be a grandmother. I was on the other side of a very large room, yet it was as if everything got noticeably quiet, and I could hear her reply which was almost a shout, "Does not look like May will have children."

Those words cut me to the core, and I immediately felt sick. That devastating frozen memory became etched in my mind. I can still see that moment, remembering everything right down to the clothes I was wearing, what the room looked like, the smells, and especially that deep, sickening feeling.

After I dropped her off that night, I earnestly prayed, "God, I am believing You as my Creator for a baby. I have asked, and I am asking again." I reminded God of His Word, "God, you said to be fruitful and multiply and that includes me. Your Word says if I delight in You, you will give me the desires of my heart. You gave Samuel to Hannah when she prayed, 'O Lord of Hosts, if Thou wilt indeed look on the affliction of thine handmaid, and remember me' (I Sam. 1:11). I said, "remember me, too."

I stood in faith. I bought baby outfits as proof I was believing. I would say affirmations that God was blessing me with a child. I was implementing steps of faith; however, I did not really understand or even know what I was doing. Yet, faith prevailed, and two weeks later I was pregnant with our son, Jonathan.

After Jonathan was born, I became pregnant again, yet I miscarried, for a total of four miscarriages. When Jonathan turned 18 months old, I started praying and working the steps for another baby. I knew if God gave me one, he could give me another one.

My second son, Jared, was born on my birthday. He was two weeks past my due date but was destined to be my 29th birthday gift.

After Jared was born, I stopped taking steps that moved me forward. I got caught up in myself once again, into loneliness, a longing for more, a state of not knowing where our lives were going. My husband, Gerald, and I were not on the same page, and instead of taking steps forward together, we ended up stepping into divorce court. It was the most heartbreaking experience I have ever gone through. I realized how quickly we can forget the steps we learn.

LESSONS AT A GLANCE

- I prayed and made my petition known. I asked for what I wanted and needed.
- I reminded my Creator of His Word. I found the scriptures I needed to confirm His will for me. If you can find it in His Word, you can have it. "For there is no respecter of persons with God" (Rom. 2:11). If He did it for one, He can for another.
- I declared my faith, stood in faith, and took actions of faith.
- Sometimes even after years of moving forward, we may stop taking steps. We may even take steps backward. It doesn't mean we are meant to be at a standstill forever.

YOUR NEXT STEPS

1. What are you believing for? Ask for it. Say a prayer and be specific about what you want. Our Creator cares about our wants, our desires, and our needs. "Ask, and it shall be given you; seek, and ye shall find; knock, and it shall be opened unto you: For everyone that asketh receiveth: and he that seeketh findeth; and to him that knocketh it shall be opened" (Matt. 7: 7-8). "If ye then, being evil, know how to give good gifts unto your children, how much more shall your Father in Heaven give good things to them that ask Him" (Matt. 7:11).

2. Look up in the Word if it is His will. You cannot ask for something that is not in the will of our Creator. Make sure it lines up with His Word. Where is it in the Bible? "Every good and every perfect gift is from above" (James 1:17). Look up the scripture you are standing on.

3. Then stand as if you already have it. What can you do to act as if it is already yours? Here is an example: buying baby clothes when believing for a baby.

4. If we do not continue to grow every day, we can find ourselves taking steps backwards instead of going forward. If you find yourself moving backwards or at a standstill, acknowledge it and make the sincere effort to take that next step in the direction you are meant to go.

CHAPTER 3

DIVORCE AND TRAUMA

I was 30 years old, devastated and broken, once again robbed of hope. I was grappling with betrayal, loss, and overwhelming uncertainty. I never actually imagined myself getting to this place. I knew deep down that our marriage was falling apart, but I kept telling myself that, somehow, we could make it work. Consciously, I did not want to admit we were failing, as I did not know how to fix it. I had conquered having an emotional affair. I had conquered becoming a mother. I was settled in the fact that I would remain married and raise these children God had given me by faith for the rest of my life.

However, at this point, I did not know I could create a life by my own design. This divorce was an entirely new place I found myself in. How was I going to conquer this one? I had loved Gerald so deeply. I heard the song, "I Fooled Around and Fell in Love" by Elvin Bishop over and over in my head. I had fallen in love, yet I was miserable and lonely, and I had no idea what steps I needed to take to continue in my marriage.

It was a very sad, emotional, trying time for me. I kept wondering if I would be better off staying. I feared the unknown that my tomorrows held for me and my boys. I ended up back at square one, wanting to dance through life, but now with no partner; yearning to be graceful while on "two left feet" again; desperately trying to figure out life.

I had so many questions. Why is this happening? What caused it? Where did I fail? What could we have done? What could I have done differently to change this outcome? I loved Gerald but felt I would be going backward, instead of forward, if we did not move on separately. Love alone was not enough.

My life and my children's lives had taken a drastic turn, I was not sure where it was going to take us. I knew that sometimes we could end up in unexpected places, such as divorce. However, I could not believe I was here.

I did not know the steps to take to overcome it. I started by seeing a counselor. He explained that if your hope is diminished, your expectations need a boost. I had to get out of the questioning state of "why" and on to what I wanted my life to look like from that point on. We must expect that with hope, all good things will come into our lives. He took me back to the basics. What is faith and how does it operate? "Now faith is the substance of things hoped for, the evidence of things not seen" (Heb. 11:1).

The counselor told me to write a list of what I wanted my life to look like. My one big requirement was that my boys had to be taken care of. I wanted a helpmate to help me raise them and to love me unconditionally. The counselor explained that faith works and will bring about what we expect, good or bad. He asked me, "What are you expecting in your life, and what are you expecting in a marriage? What are you expecting for your children and for your dreams?" Basically, he had me dig deep to understand what my life would look like if I were to design it myself.

The counselor picked up on so many wounds within me and recommended that I see a therapist to become the real me; to get free from the baggage of childhood fears and of my failed marriage. Those fears – plus the hiding and the non-confrontational attitude I had – are what contributed to my walking away from our marriage instead of hitting it head-on and trying to save it. I had become very co-dependent and lost my identity. He explained this change needed to happen before I allowed myself to get into another relationship or it could very possibly fail, as well.

The therapist immediately recognized I had lost myself in my journey of life. He called me out on my need to rediscover my authentic self. "You are a hider, a person who does not want to be seen. You must get out from behind the door and enjoy life," he told me. I couldn't understand how he knew all of that.

He identified the fear that was deep-seated in me from growing up and experiencing my father having PTSD-related raging fits as a result of his war experiences. Dad would throw tea jugs, glasses, and ashtrays, not meaning to harm anyone, but trying to alleviate the pain he was experiencing. The fits, the things he broke, and the energy that came along with that had set up a profound fear in me, and the easiest response was to hide and remain unseen.

I got good at hiding. I did not like confrontations or anyone getting loud. I carried this fear into my marriage, yet I had no clue. I thought that since I was with my dad a lot in my teenage years and grew to love him with a deep love, all the fear had been released. But I discovered I had only hidden it. My mother had explained to me the real man she married and how the war had affected him, and my compassion for him grew.

As a child, I did not understand what he was going through; however, after suffering emotional pain myself, I got a glimpse of the pain he experienced. I realized that pain hurts your core, no matter how it comes or what causes it.

I will never forget the night Dad passed away from lung cancer, with my mother and all eight of his children at his side. That was the night I knew I had to forgive him, and I thought I had. However, the fear remained. He passed peacefully, but just before he passed, he looked in all our eyes with so much love and said, "I love you. There is a God, and I want to see all of you again one day." It was a devastating moment for a 16-year-old, but it started my journey of wanting to pursue a deeper relationship with my Creator, as I wanted to see my dad again someday.

The therapist had gotten to the core of the pain and explained that it needed to be dealt with, otherwise it would always remain. I had to get out from behind the door and let the fear go. I finally let it go after writing a letter to my dad explaining the fear that the behavior I experienced had caused. I burned the letter and totally released myself from all the fear, as well as the non-confrontational attitude that it had caused in me.

I began to realize the immense power in releasing forgiveness. I had to forgive my ex-husband; he had given the marriage all he could give. He also had wounds he had brought to our marriage. He could only give what he had been given.

I had to forgive myself for getting a divorce, for quitting on the man whom I adored and genuinely loved. I had to forgive myself for not feeling good enough, for not being my true self, even though I did not know how to be. I had to forgive myself for not knowing how to go through life. That one really beat me up. I had prayed for children and was given them, but I had no clue how to manage my life, much less how to be a good wife or a good mother. I am thankful for the lessons of forgiveness I was able to learn.

Post-separation from Gerald, once I realized how Dad's anger had taught me to be a hider and the way this approach had affected my marriage, I knew I had to let go of blame, shame, negativity, and anger. I had to find myself and create a new mindset. If such things are not released and a person leaves one relationship without behavior changes, such patterns will likely be repeated in subsequent relationships.

It took work, but I created a new mindset as I healed from the divorce and the pain of the past.

Before I could move forward, there were other things I needed to learn: every day, life is either happening *to* us or life is happening *for* us. If life is working against us – giving us unwanted gifts and unwanted lessons – then, perhaps, our language needs to change. Our attitudes may need to change, as well. Either we are not taking the steps we need to take, or our actions, our belief systems need updating, as my therapist said.

The therapist explained how we get stuck in life when we think, "Why is this happening to me, why am I here, why am I so sad? Why, why, why?" To get unstuck, we must change our mindset to, "Why is this happening *for* me? What lesson do I need to learn? What steps am I missing? What direction am I going in with my attitude, my thoughts, or my visions?"

I also had to let go of shame. I was wasting time living in my yesterdays. I needed to release all those questions – what could I have done? What should I have done? -and live in the day. The past is the past. Let the past stay behind you.

We must be in a beautiful state to get out of the negative state. No one can do that for us. Our children will reflect on our state. If we are down in the dumps and lost, where will our children be? Down in the dumps and lost, as well.

I had to figure out what I wanted my life and my children's lives to be like. This one was extremely hard. I had to design my life and I had no clue how.

After being separated from my husband for four months, I re-alized he had only called a couple of times to check on us, and he had not provided any money to buy essentials. I filed for a divorce.

When Gerald got the divorce papers, he asked me to reconcile. It was another earth-shattering moment, yet I said "No!" I felt that I would be taking steps backward, and I was not where I could try again, mentally, or emotionally. I told him our bridge had washed out, and I couldn't swim. It was a moment I debat-ed many times afterwards: "Did I make a right decision?" His reply to me that day was a truly selfless statement: "I love you enough to let you find your happiness."

I am not an advocate for divorce. If you once loved each other enough to marry, I believe it is quite possible to love each other enough to work through and make the marriage work.

I do wish I had understood "how-to steps" back then. No partner will ever be perfect, and neither will we be. We all have flaws we must work on. I believe that couples should always remember the "til death do us part" line of their wedding vows. I remembered that part, and that was why I had such a hard time coming to terms with the divorce. I did not know how to be real, authentic, or vulnerable. I did not know how to communicate what I needed. Heck, I did not even know what I needed. I feel so many marriages end this way. Had I known, my life and my children's lives would have been different.

However, if abuse is present in the marriage, you must get out.

LESSONS AT A GLANCE

✴ Counselors and therapists can help us get to the root of our issues. They helped me acknowledge that I was hiding. It was a pivotal awakening in my life and my ability to take the necessary steps.

✴ A big part of finding my authentic self was forgiveness toward others and myself. It allowed me to release pain and issues that I was not even consciously aware of.

✴ Letting go of negative feelings and a mindset rooted in the past allows us to be open minded for the future.

✴ Divorce is not always the answer, and communication and authenticity can save a marriage, unless abuse is present.

YOUR NEXT STEPS

1. If your hope is diminished, look into meeting with a counselor, your pastor, a coach, or someone who can dig into helping you renew it. Seek someone who is trained in giving guidance on your situation.

2. If a counselor recommends a therapist, be open to seeing one. They can dig in and find core issues. Write down what you think is your core issue. Oftentimes, we already know in our subconscious. Writing can help us uncover it.

3. Let go of shame and blame and, more importantly, forgive. Make a list of everyone who wronged you, or whom you have wronged. Forgive them and let it go. Write them a letter, and if you cannot get it to the person or if doing so would cause more harm, just burn it after writing it. It still allows you to go through that process and forgive.

4. Focus on recreating your life by your design. What life would you design for yourself and your family? Write it down and be specific about where you would like to be. I suggest one-year, three-year, and five-year goals to stay on track.

CHAPTER 4

PERSISTENCE PAYS OFF

After things get messy in life, we can rediscover the persistence to move forward. Joe was divorced when we met. His marriage was also dysfunctional. They had been married almost 16 years and had twins – a boy and a girl. He said it was a very hard decision, but they knew the best thing for all parties involved was to dissolve their marriage.

I had prayed for God to send me a helpmate to raise my boys with me. Then Joe came along; we worked together at a local Goodyear plant. He would come around quite often to talk to me, and we became friends. One day, he asked me if he could buy me coffee, and I simply replied, "I do not drink coffee." I was not interested.

Still, he persisted. He continued to come around, talking about his children with such love for them, and talking about the lady he had started seeing. We chatted about anything that friends would typically talk about. We laughed together, sharing funny stories. We even talked about the guy I had started seeing at the time.

Several ladies I worked with had formed a Goodyear bowling league and I would go bowling every Thursday with them. The ladies and I would meet up before we bowled to eat breakfast.

Joe asked if he could tag along. I assumed it was because he knew a couple of the ladies he'd gone to school with. I was so naive. We would laugh and have a good time, but I never once suspected he was there to see me.

We continued building a friendship for over a year. One day he said, "I am never giving up on you." I laughed, and I still did not know why he stayed so persistent. I was not attracted to him. You may have thought about who you felt your perfect match would be and have had an image in your mind. I did ... and Joe was not it. He was much shorter than I envisioned. He did not seem like the guy I could fall in love with. Boy, was I wrong! About six months after that, I finally agreed to go out with him. His persistence had finally won.

It is funny because when I finally agreed to go out with him, he said he turned around and asked himself, "Oh crap. What do I do now?"

Looking back, I see how Joe worked the steps. He had a mindset of being determined to go out with me, used a skillset of talking and engaging with me, committed to a strategy of repeating it, and persisted in implementing his actions. After all my reluctance over that time, all it took was one date, and I knew he was someone I could fall in love with. It has been 31 years since then, and we are still in love.

Less than a year after that first date, we were married. He was everything I wanted: a man to share my life with, and a loving, family-oriented man, at that. He wanted to raise our children in church, as that was one of the most important things to me. He was my type of guy, after all. He had passion for life, he loved to take vacations, he loved laughter, he loved me, and he loved my children. I grew to truly love him, and I even grew to love coffee.

We have always had the same values, same goals, and same passions, and together we have had lots of fun. Granted, our life has been amazing, but that doesn't mean we didn't go through a serious rough patch to get there.

When Joe and I married, Chris and Lori were 11, Jonathan was 5, and Jared was 2. I had often wondered what he was thinking, taking on a wife with two small children, yet I hadn't even contemplated what I was thinking, taking on 11-year-old twins. While we knew it would be a challenge to blend our families, we had no clue how hard it would actually be. With no instruction manual and no idea what would come next, we were in for quite a ride.

LESSONS AT A GLANCE

✳ Sometimes what we envision for our life is not entirely accurate.

✳ We may need to be open, not just with our needs and desires for our lives, but open to the notion that things might be different than we expect and yet exactly what we are meant to have.

✳ Faith and persistence can win; it may take time, patience, and understanding.

YOUR NEXT STEPS

1. Think about what you want for your life. Get the picture in your mind, write it down, and make a vision board. Put it where you can see it regularly.

2. Be open to recognizing that things may not always be given to you exactly how you expect. Make a consistent effort to be open minded.

3. Keep your faith in place.

4. Stay persistent in your stand, even when the doubts come. When you question things, keep standing, holding your head high and trusting in the future.

5. Know that YOU WILL WIN!

CHAPTER 5

WHEN TWO FAMILIES BECOME ONE

At the time Joe and his wife separated, Chris wanted to move in with him, but the judge said that he would have to wait until he was about 12. Less than six months into our marriage, the twins reached that age, and the judge spoke with Chris and awarded custody to Joe. We knew we had to stick together, but we had no clue how hard it would be or how many steps it would take to merge our family. We had no choice but to dive in and make it work.

We quickly learned that if one parent in the home said one thing, it had to be as though both parents were talking. We could not let the kids "play us." As far as the rules were concerned, Joe enforced them and would communicate with his ex-wife what was happening, so she could enforce the same rules. Doing this made it hard for the children to play the parents with all the "he said, she said."

Kids are often smarter than you think, but I have to say all parents involved did the best they could under the circumstances. The twins would try to play Joe and his ex-wife on occasion, but if found out, it would not work. Sometimes it was found out after the fact though, and the kids did what they wanted due to miscommunication. We found how necessary clear communication was in keeping things running smoothly.

Through our biggest hurdles, we were quick to learn we had to stick together, no matter what. We continually tried to look for ways to make it through the intense times and we had many. The kids would try to play each parent, the stepparents, and anyone else they could manipulate to get what they wanted. We stuck together, even if we felt the other parent was being too hard or was wrong. We would discuss how we felt in private and never in front of the children.

In our home, on birthdays and Christmases, if one child got something, they all got something equivalent. Shopping for clothes was the same way.

I grounded Chris for a month once because of his smart mouth. It started out as one week, and he kept on with his backtalk and his rudeness, so then it went to two, then three, and by the time he stopped he was grounded for four weeks. Joe and I stuck it out together. It was rough, but we made believers out of the kids. No matter what, they were to learn they could not play us against each other. We knew staying committed to taking the necessary steps would keep us on the same page to make it work. That is key in any marriage. Anyone committed can and will make it happen if they choose to stick together.

Joe and I found many of the answers we sought in the Bible, as it was given to us by our Heavenly Father. We chose to stay close to our Heavenly Father so we would not lose our way on this journey of parenting and merging our families. The Word says let us not grow weary in well-doing. Raising children can make you weary. Stay the course, be persistent, and you will reap in due season!

While it's certainly a moment-by-moment journey bringing families together and tackling the issues as they arise, we recognized that a few key tactics were crucial. The determination to work together and stay on the same page, to have consistent open communication, and to stand our ground on what we felt was best for us all as a family was vital in merging as successfully as possible.

LESSONS AT A GLANCE

✳ Parents need to stick together and stay on the same page, especially during conflict when the children try to test their boundaries and manipulate the parents.

✳ Lines of communication must remain open between parents in the household, as well as with each child's other biological parent.

✳ Clear communication with the children is also important so they know what is considered acceptable behavior and understand the consequences of their actions.

✳ It is important to treat the children equally, giving them equal gifts, as well as equal attention and love.

✳ Many answers can be found in the Bible.

YOUR NEXT STEPS

1. Depending on which stage you are in, write down steps you feel you and your spouse should take in your family merger. If you are not in a family merger, write down steps that you feel you can take to strengthen the family dynamic in your household.

2. Make a conscious effort to stay on the same playing field as your spouse. Remember that you are a team when disciplining and instilling values in your children.

3. Be real with your spouse on a level that he/she can understand. Openly discuss any parenting conflicts or family issues together. Your lives and your children's lives depend on your merger.

4. Be mindful when communicating your expectations for your children.

CHAPTER 6

STEPCHILDREN'S DISRESPECT

My persistence was tried very quickly. Children in a blend can be difficult and disrespectful, all the while still needing love in order to become successful adults. Our next steps were to learn how to overcome the hurdles of the children's behavior. On top of learning how to thrive as a family. The struggle was getting real.

I heard, "I hate you," my stepson, Chris, exclaimed to me as loudly as he could. I heard that more than once. He had moved in with us quickly after the marriage and was such a sweet child at the beginning. At the wedding, he had looked at me with loving, bright green eyes and a huge smile and said, "If my dad was not marrying you, I sure would." That would soon change. The stability of the blend was about to be tried, and we had a lot to learn.

His twin sister, Lori, was content living with her mom and coming over when she could. They both were active in sports, and it worked out that we would do the running with him, and her mom did the running for her. We would catch each child's events when the schedules didn't conflict.

In my mind, this should have been great: three boys and a girl, and a sweet, loving, caring man by my side. What more could I want? I was elated. I now had four children that I could pour my heart into. For a brief while, I felt complete. However, it was not long until I discovered it was not great at all. I was in a whirlwind of emotions. I had a new husband and children whom I had no clue how to manage. By that time, Jonathan was 6, Jared was 3, and the twins were 12.

Chris thought he was the boss. He was very disrespectful, smart mouthed, and annoyed that his dad had someone else in his life. At the same time, he was still that loving, green-eyed boy, and he also needed love. I remember one day he was being very disrespectful and smart-mouthed to me. I do not believe in, nor do I approve of slapping a child in the face; however, that day I slapped him before I even knew what I had done. He looked at me, shocked, and said, "You had better never slap me again! You are not my mother!"

My response was, "You had better never talk to me like that again! I am not your mother, you have a mother, and I am not trying to replace her. If one day we can be friends, that would be great, but while in my home, you will respect me!"

It was clear he did not like me, and at that point, I did not like him, either. I had enough of him. I looked at my husband when he got home and told him I was leaving and that I was not cut out to be a stepmom. I said, "I love you, but I cannot tolerate this pain." I had experienced pain in the earlier marriage and was not going to settle into another life of such distress. I felt I could not stay there living with this child, and it was not fair to Joe to have to choose between me and his son. It was unfair for the other kids to go through more pain, as well.

In his ever-so-soft tone, he quietly told me, "We will work this out." He asked the magic question, "How do we make this work?" The answer showed up and became clear. A lot of times we gripe, we groan, we complain, but we never ask the right questions that will get the correct answers to show up. We get too stuck in ourselves. Anyone self-absorbed and unable to focus on a solution will never find the answer.

Have you heard this comment: "If you focus on the rear-view mirror, you will go in the ditch or – even worse – hit a tree or another vehicle." It is true that where our focus goes, our energy flows. That energy flow will cause something to happen. It may be good, or it may be bad.

Joe was in this marriage to stay. He was persistent. I was not. I was not sure I wanted to stay. I wanted not only to walk, but I was eager to run away as fast as I could. Joe said we would one day be old people on the front porch, watching the sunsets and remembering our life together. I thought there was no way that would ever happen. I wanted out!

Thankfully, Joe was humble and sincere, and with a gesture of pure love towards me, he suggested we get family counseling. We needed answers and we knew we needed to find them quickly. I went along with his idea grudgingly since I had gone through extensive counseling after my divorce, and I was not prepared for more.

The counselor was so wise. He told us to set boundaries to live in our home. He told us to write a list of rules that would be enforced for anyone who wanted to live in our house. He also told us to have Chris write a list of rules he would have to abide by to live in our house. We would then compare them and produce a list upon which we could all agree. When we were given Chris' list of rules, we found they were surprisingly stricter than our own. It was then I discovered this child wanted boundaries and security, as all children do. He wanted to know he mattered.

Some rules that were on the list, which we still abide by, are:

* ❊ Dinner at 6 p.m., unless other obligations are set for that time, such as ball games or other outings and events.

* ❊ Church on Sundays.

* ❊ Chores for each child.

* ❊ If a child is grounded at our home, he or she is grounded in the other parent's home as well, depending on the grounding level.

* ❊ Different levels of consequences per occurrence are in place when it comes to breaking a boundary. For example, as a first time for back-talking consequence, the child must write "I will not back-talk" numerous times. The second time the child breaks a boundary, they may lose a privilege such as having someone over to spend the night or using the phone. The third time, they would be grounded from going anywhere such as ballgames, or to friend's outings.

Once the list is drawn up and signed by all children, it MUST be enforced. Only when children know the list will stand – regardless of begging, pleading, or throwing a fit – harmony will begin in the home.

Those rules were applied in our family, and all the children brought up in our home, from that day forward, lived by the rules and were disciplined by the rules. They knew they were loved by the rules, as well. Implementation of these steps truly works. Fast forward from the time we first created and enforced the lists: now when adult Chris calls me on the phone, he says, "What's up, Mom?" He turned out to be a son whom I love, and I am proud to call him mine.

Our lives took a vastly different turn from what they could have been. The conflict ended; harmony came into our home. Chris and I became remarkably close. He is not only my son, but, amazingly, he is also my friend. We agree on so many levels that it is hard to believe we ever had conflicts or that he is not my biological child.

I am happy to say, I was able to stick it out. The early grueling days were not pretty, nor were they what I expected for my life, but I am so thankful for Joe, through it all. Without his firm stand and persistence, I – once again – would have walked away, and I would then have missed out on an amazing life.

LESSONS AT A GLANCE

- It is important to ask the right questions. For us, it was Joe asking, "How do we make this work?"
- Our answer was getting family counseling from an expert and taking that expert's advice. If I hadn't been willing to try, the trajectory of my life would have been very different.
- Setting and enforcing boundaries that were aligned with all our needs and expectations was key to putting a stop to the conflict.
- Harmony is attainable when communication is open, and all parties involved make an effort.

YOUR NEXT STEPS

1. Take inventory: Are you parenting together, or are the children parenting? Are you sticking together in your decisions? Take a hard look and see what you may need to correct or redirect in the best interest of the children and for harmony in the household.

2. Be open to family counseling if your home is out of hand, as mine was. Looking through a counselor's lens can be extremely helpful.

3. Write a "Must List" for living in your home. Set boundaries that are signed by each family member. Outline the consequences for each offense. Know that your list will be unique to your family.

4. Once the list is written and signed by all children (and parents), it MUST be enforced. Once the children know the list will stand regardless of begging, pleading, or throwing a fit, harmony will begin in the home.

CHAPTER 7

BECOMING A STEPSON

This is Chris' story of how he learned the steps to becoming not just a stepson, but one who I am proud to call my son. It is his journey of becoming an overcomer, learning lessons of boundaries, and becoming close to his Creator.

Chris Shares His Story

"This weekend I want you to meet someone," my dad said. I questioned who and he replied, "A friend. We are eating at her house in Hornbeak." I did not think too much about it, other than that it was a little strange. A couple of weeks before, another friend was helping me recover from the chicken pox.

My parents had divorced, and I consciously decided I wanted nothing to do with these new relationships or family closeness. My parents had a toxic relationship, and, in turn, my twin sister and I responded in the same way towards each other. I was about to find out that my definition of love was not what it was supposed to be.

We pulled up to May's house with the purple paint and pink shutters, which were actually gray paint and mauve shutters, but they sure looked purple to me. I remember thinking, "This is a first." From the beginning, I sensed something different about this woman. She had a genuine smile and a caring personality. Attentive, it was like her eyes enlarged and bugged out as she would move in closer as I talked to her. Weird.

She had this joyful singing that came along with whatever she was doing (and still does). I called them Jesus' songs. She sang while she finished cooking the spaghetti and had huge, delicious, yeast rolls that I had never seen or eaten before. They were so good. Not long after we met her, they married.

I knew May was genuine. Whatever it was that was different about her, I knew deep down that I liked it. My curiosity about God began to intensify. In my heart, I knew I wanted to live with my father, but I did not want to cause pain for my mother. The decision was difficult, discomforting, and my thoughts were very troubling. Finally, I was allowed to move in with him.

My attraction to this new stepmother soon changed. It was not at all what I was expecting. This woman came with control. I came with resistance. She stayed consistent in her beliefs and who she was. She took away some of my freedoms that I had while living with my mother. Church was necessary to her. If I was not home on Sunday mornings, I had better find a service somewhere. We had many disagreements, from the friends I spent time with, to the television shows I watched, to the music I listened to (which she gracefully took away).

She even introduced me to a slap in the face for my disrespectful mouth, which escalated my ill feelings toward her. I hated her at the time. It became an all-out war. She was not happy with me, and I sure was not happy with her. We had a problem that desperately needed to be fixed.

I learned change can come, but not without resistance. May stood her ground with me. She was then, and still is, a God-fearing, living example. She treated me as her own. Thirty-one years have passed, and I have grown up. We made it. Today we have an unexplained closeness, a closeness I wish we had had years ago. She is no longer May. Instead, I call her "Mom." I love her and am so thankful that she stayed in our lives.

May was right, she said she would never be my mom; I had a mom. However, she did not say I could not have two moms. As I reflect and share, I am not trying to paint the picture as if our lives were always bad. The opposite is true.

My family life was everything I wanted it to be, both of my parents and my stepmother were very loving and supportive, always wanting the best for me. Through life's normal struggles and bad decisions, it was I who chose to distance myself from them. However, I was never without parents encouraging me to change my path when I was headed in a wrong direction. They would alert me when they saw I was being triggered. I came to realize they knew me more than I knew myself.

I had to learn the hard way; triggers can get a person in a very bad spot. I wish I had learned early on to listen to them. I fell a lot of times and had to get myself back together, if only I had listened. My parents were smarter than I realized.

Brokenness within families is common. It is a life-changing factor and, unless handled properly, it can destroy lives. Throughout my own brokenness, a wonderful woman was placed in my life. I became a stepparent myself. I quickly realized the pressures and the difficulties that go along with it. I found myself asking my stepmother for advice. Ironic how life turns around for you and the hand you tried to do without is the hand that helps you.

Their mother and I are no longer together. However, I trust and believe Romans 8:28: "And we know that all things work for good to them that love God, to them who are called according to his purpose." My biological daughter, my two stepdaughters, and I are all close. I know we will have that closeness the rest of our lives. We had the example set for us.

I have learned empathy, compassion, and helplessness, all at the same time, as I have watched others who have floundered around in their messes and lost their way, as I have. I am still learning. I have learned we need mentors. We need to lean on others to help when we cannot figure it out, or we will get ourselves in more messes, and I have several times.

We also need accountability partners, as they will be a big help if you let them hold you accountable. We all have rough patches to go through in life, but trusting and having those around you who keep you focused are both necessary. I would say they are a must.

Faith is sometimes all I had, and I was weak in that too many times. I wish I had strengthened my faith more deeply and understood this when I was young, instead of waiting until I was older. I wish I had learned to be vulnerable and transparent sooner. I could have saved myself a lot of heartache.

I am thankful for my parents who have stood and encouraged me through my journey. I know that my future will be better than my past. I love the scripture, "For I know the thoughts that I think toward you, saith the Lord, thoughts of peace, and not of evil, to give you an expected end" (Jer. 29:11). That is my hope and my stand. "The one thing that has kept me going throughout my struggles in life is knowing God has plans for me, to give me hope and a future." I know my Creator knows the end from the beginning, even when we cannot see the end, He can.

LESSONS AT A GLANCE

- To fix a problem, you must acknowledge that it exists and needs fixing.
- Change can come, although often with resistance.
- Becoming a stepparent gives you a greater understanding of the bigger picture.
- Sometime those you try to do without can become the ones who help you the most.
- You are always learning, and it is important to have mentors, accountability partners, hope, and faith along the journey.

YOUR NEXT STEPS

1. If you have a problem that needs to be fixed, identify it. Getting out of denial is the first step.

2. Commit to the change and the steps to make the change, knowing that resistance is likely.

3. Accept where you are. Identify where you want to go. Ask what you need to get there. You can ask your Creator "How?" Then, listen.

4. If you are struggling, find a coach, a counselor, a therapist, a mentor, or an accountability partner to help you get back on track.

5. Continue to learn and to strengthen your faith muscles. Faith can carry you far if you can only believe. Remind yourself daily, "I know God has plans for me to give me hope and a future."

CHAPTER 8

THE LESSONS PASS ON

Jonathan was 5 when Joe and I married. He was the sweetest little brown-haired, blue-eyed boy. He loved me and gave the greatest hugs a mom could ever want. He was my first-born, and the bond we had was special. He was a desire of my heart manifested because I would not give up.

As a baby, he would stare at me so intently. It was like he was looking at me with a depth I had never seen. He had moved into a part of my heart that would always be only his "my first-born." I understood how the smallest things can take up a huge part of your heart.

He was a great child growing up – always learning and display-ing leadership qualities. He was the strongest-willed child in our home. He would argue his point and would win. He could get us to see his point very easily. I always thought he would be a great lawyer with his persuasiveness. He had an uncanny way with words, and he still does. We had many conversations. Even as a child, when he spoke, he amazed me with his deep perception.

Jonathan had bonded with his biological dad, and it was very painful for him when we divorced. The blend required some adjusting on Jonathan's part, as well, because Joe's parenting wisdom was different from what the rest of us were used to. I remember one day not long after we were married, Joe was teaching Jonathan to be an avid fisherman and hunter. Jonathan went to the pond almost every day.

One day, after he returned without his fishing pole, Joe asked, "Jonathan, where is your fishing pole?" Joe reminded Jonathan a couple of weeks prior, we had to take one of our horses to the veterinarian to remove a fishhook from his hoof. He told him to go down to the pond and get the fishing pole. It was getting dark by this time, and we did not have lights by the pond.

My mother came apart. "He is not going out there in the dark," she exclaimed. She was going to go get it herself. Joe intervened and stopped her. "He will forget it again if he does not go get it himself," he said. Jonathan headed to the pond, flashlight in hand. His predominant emotion of anger overshadowed his fear. On the other hand, Maw-Maw was outraged.

The journey of understanding children and grandparents began. A blend involves more than the children and the parents. It affects grandparents, too. At that time, both Joe and I worked third shift at the former Goodyear plant in Union City. Mom would stay with the kids while we worked and go home the next morning. That day, she exclaimed, "I will stay tonight, but you will need to get someone else tomorrow!" She was so hurt to see a little frightened and angry boy being made to go out in the dark to get his fishing pole.

We went to work not knowing how she would be when we got home. The next morning, she was calm, and she told Joe she was sorry for acting as she had. She said she realized he was right. She knew if Joe had not made Jonathan get the fishing pole, it would have kept on happening. Lesson learned.

If something is recurring in your life and you are responding the same way over and over, you need to break the cycle. Do an interrupt, stop the pattern, and watch what happens. In our case, Jonathan did not leave a fishing pole at the pond after that. In addition, Joe and Mom grew a bond from that day forward. She knew Joe had the best intentions for the children. She stayed with us, helping with our children while we worked. She told the boys stories, read the Bible to them, and played cards and games with all of us.

Over the years, Jonathan collaborated with Joe and me in business endeavors and was our right hand in a couple of restaurants we owned. He was a big asset to us. He was preparing to go to college in East Tennessee, and he kept telling me when he left, "Joe will be shutting down the restaurant." We had come too far in this restaurant to shut it down. Joe had already closed one of the restaurants because it was not profitable, but the other one was successful. I did not believe Jonathan, so I just shook off his comment.

I learned that, oftentimes, our children know what they are talking about. Two weeks after Jonathan left, Joe closed the restaurant. I cried for the next two weeks following it. I lost Jonathan to college, we closed the restaurant, and I had so much uncertainty. Where would my next steps take me? It ended up being a great decision on Joe's part, since restaurant work is extremely hard, but at the time, it was not something I could see clearly.

Today, Jonathan is highly successful. I am so proud of my strong-willed child. He is still close with his dad, and he loves Joe as well. Jonathan is married to Tabitha; she is as strong-willed as he is. That strong will has kept them together through struggles and hardships. They built a house beside us, and we love having our two grandchildren in our home almost every day.

A funny thing happened not long ago. Jonathan's son, my 10-year-old grandson, Jon Carter, walked by me, and I asked him, "Where are you going?" Disgusted, he replied, "To the pond to get my fishing pole." He had gone home, and his dad was sending him back to the pond to get his fishing pole. The same lesson Jonathan had learned years before was now being passed along to his son.

LESSONS AT A GLANCE

- A blend involves more than kids and parents. It can greatly affect grandparents, as well.
- Break the cycle if something negative is recurring in your life.
- Listen to children. A lot of times, they know what they are talking about.
- The same lessons we learned have a way of influencing our own children and grandchildren.

YOUR NEXT STEPS

1. Be mindful of others who engage in your children's lives, whether grandparents, uncles, aunts, or cousins. Never take their comments personally. Try to see things from their perspective when this is needed.

2. If something is recurring in your life and you are doing the same thing over and over, break the cycle. Do an interrupt, change the pattern, and watch what happens. Even a simple reset can have positive and lasting effects.

3. Listen intently to your children. Oftentimes they may see truths that we do not necessarily agree with and are unable to make sense of, at first. Make it a point to have open communication to avoid overlooking opportunities to understand.

CHAPTER 9

BONDING AND VALUABLE LESSONS LEARNED

This is Jonathan's story of his journey, and how he learned to bond with his stepdad. He learned many lessons to pass on to others to have a thriving life.

Jonathan Shares His Story

I was 5 years old when my mom married my stepdad, Joe. Jared and I could not have asked for a better stepdad. He has shown true loyalty, not only to my mother, but to all of us: his children, Jared and me, and the children he and my mother adopted. He has been the best example to all of us that working hard, loving hard, giving hard, and living a life of passion pays off.

Joe taught us how to have fun like riding horses, camping out, going on several vacations, and making memories together. He taught me things I might not have learned without him in my life – things like hunting, fishing, carpentry, and mechanics. He even taught me how to run a restaurant and convinced me that I will never own one; there's too much demanding work. However, I will say that I am a good cook because of him. Ribs are my specialty.

Joe also taught us about things we did not like to do, such as working. He built our house and, yes, even at an early age, we had to help. When he built our shop, we had to help. Any job he was doing, if we could help, he had us helping him. I did not appreciate it growing up, but what I gained was worth much more than all those times I was unhappy about it. A few years ago, we built my house, and I am thankful for the knowledge he passed on to me. In addition, Joe also has a calm coolness about him that I see in all the boys. He definitely rubbed off on all of us.

I had a bond with my biological father as I was growing up, and I tried to communicate with him as much as I could. He was a truck driver and I remember going with him on the road a few times. My brother did not communicate with him like I did, and I could not understand why. It caused a lot of needless pain between us for years.

I was learning to bond with Joe; however, it was hard because I had a strong bond with my biological dad. I had to learn that I could be loyal to both my dad and to Joe. The biggest lesson I learned is a bond can never be forced on anyone. It was not until I had children that I understood how the bond works.

I have always had a bond with my mother. I did not understand her thinking at times, but I highly respected her in everything she did. She had several things she endeavored and was/is a forever learner, and I have a much better understanding of her now that I have gotten older. She taught me valuable lessons, such as always to pursue my best self and to stay committed to

God and family. She always worked hard, and she showed us that life will give you rewards.

After having children of my own, I could not imagine anyone contributing to their lives other than their mother and me. We have had storms come through that tried to break us up. But through the storms, we made a commitment to raise them together. We did not want anyone else to raise them. She, too, had come from a blended family and had missed out on a lot with her dad as she grew older. We did not want that for our children. Marriage is not always easy, but my wife and I are committed to each other and to our children.

My mother had a large family, and I watched as one sibling passed away after another. Through it all, my mother maintained her stability and her trust in God. She passed that emotional stability, or the emotional handicap, as some would call it, on to her children. When others are strong, sometimes it is hard to grasp that what they are displaying is emotional stability, not lack of love. I can say my mother absolutely loved her family, and they loved her.

She stayed true to her family and still has the gatherings at her house. She taught us that family matters. She had birthdays, Thanksgiving, July 4th celebrations, any special occasion that arose, and Christmas meals with her family around our table as far back as I can remember. There was always a full house. My grandmother and my mother's six siblings (one had already passed before I was born) spent time at our house. We were so blessed to have had not only my grandmother but also our aunts and uncles in our lives. The memories are priceless. She now has only one sibling left. As each aunt and uncle passed away, I began to realize just how priceless those memories really are.

A few years ago, I started the tradition with my dad's family and now we have Thanksgiving and Christmas at my house. Thankfully, they are not the size of my mom's family. Regardless of the size, my mom was right, family is so important.

LESSONS AT A GLANCE

* It can take time and effort for bonds to form and strengthen.

* When some people do not communicate and bond, it can cause others pain if they do not understand. However, bonds cannot be forced.

* We learn valuable lessons growing up that can affect how we show up as adults, in relationships, and as parents.

* Memories are priceless, even if they are not perfect.

YOUR NEXT STEPS

1. Find out what acts of love the children in your life need and desire. Whether it is devoting quality time to different activities, giving your undivided attention and being present, providing hugs, or just affirming them with kind words, these acts are vitally important and necessary in a child's life.

2. If your child has conflict with others, get to the root of it. Know that with persistence, effort, and time, bonds can strengthen, if they are meant to.

3. Schedule family time for bonding and establish traditions within the family. Life happens, and time goes quickly, so make the most of the time to create priceless memories.

CHAPTER 10

MEMORIES AND MAGIC

Jared was the cutest blonde-haired, blue-eyed baby. He looked so much like Jonathan when he was born. He was born on my 29th birthday, and what a birthday present he was! Another place was molded in my heart for Jared, "my gift." At the time I did not know what we were about to face, and I did not realize how much I needed this gift.

Jared was 6 months old when his dad and I separated. His dad was out on the road working and was not present very much during the pregnancy or during those first six months of Jared's life. He did not form a bond with him as he had with Jonathan. As previously mentioned, Jonathan grieved for his dad for years and tried to grow the bond between Jared and Gerald. It caused Jared a lot of grief, as well, because they fought for years over this. It was all due to the fact that one had bonded, and one had not.

Accepting that while the road can be rocky, we can come to understand and strengthen the bonds. My mother stepped in, feeling she needed to take his dad's place and try to "fill the void." She tried to fill my mothering role, as well, since she had so much compassion for both boys. She called Jared her "sugar baby." At times, I even had to remind her they were mine, not hers. My mother made extra time for the boys and was consciously present for them.

Jared did not talk much until he was over 2 years old. Joe is the one who got him to verbally communicate. Jared would point at something, and Joe would not give it to him until he said what he wanted. He could talk, it was simply easier for Maw-Maw to just give it to him.

Jared was 2 1/2 when Joe and I married, so he adjusted better than the other children, as he was the youngest. He grew close to Joe, as Joe was present for the boys and gave them much-needed attention. Thanks to Joe's love, care, and the safe environment he provided, the boys developed trust in their stepfather, forming a strong and meaningful bond with him.

I always believed the scripture, "For I will contend with him that contendeth with thee, and I will save thy children (Isa. 49:25)." I stood on this scripture, and I trusted God would save my children. I had trusted God for me to even have children; now I had to trust Him to help me in raising them.

I knew that even though Jared had not bonded with his biological dad, all things would work together for his good. Over time, he grew close to his dad. Wisdom comes with age, and Jared and Gerald have a good relationship now.

While establishing the bond in our blended family took time, I realized that one of the things that really helped bring us together was engaging in our children's interests. With Jared, it was anything and everything sports related. Starting at just 5 years old, he could tell us all about the games and players.

It was no surprise when he announced he was accepted to the University of Tennessee. We all loved watching Peyton Manning together during his years there. Our interest in their interests helped strengthen the connection between us all, not to mention that it created lifelong memories.

Our little sports enthusiast has grown into an amazing man. He was the oldest child to marry. His wife, Catherine, is a precious lady, whom we adore. She is a UT graduate, and she, too, loves the Tennessee Vols (a requirement in our family). Jared wanted to be completely certain before he said, "I do." He knew what it was like to have split parents and never wanted his future children to go through what he experienced. Jared and Catherine just had our 10th grandchild. I can say that being blessed, highly favored, and grace-filled have been part of our lives. God is faithful, and He has proved it.

Another gift of the journey came in June 2022; magic happened. Jared turned 33, and I turned 62. We celebrated our birthdays together at Disney World. When Jared was born, I never dreamed our lives would look like they have; however, magic showed up and our lives turned out magical, for sure.

LESSONS AT A GLANCE

❈ Some children will adjust better than others in a blended family.

❈ A bond can form with time, love, and consistency.

❈ Allow children to grow; wisdom comes with age.

❈ Parents' decisions can affect children in their lifelong decisions.

❈ Through it all, magic can happen. Sometimes we just need to recognize it.

YOUR NEXT STEPS

1. If anyone in your life is overstepping boundaries as far as that person's role in your children's lives or your own, politely – yet firmly – set up and enforce boundaries. Healthy boundaries are essential for everyone in the blend.

2. When looking to strengthen a bond, recognize that with love, nurturing, and time, the bond can happen. Seek ways of connection through shared interests, or even by learning something new together.

3. Do your part to share the wisdom you learn as you age. Take time to become familiar with the wisdom you want your children to obtain from you, and if this includes learning from your mistakes, be open and honest about it.

4. Seek the magic. It is found within the moments of laughter, the memories, and the times that we're learning, growing, and bonding, and we may not even be aware of it.

CHAPTER 11

THE EFFECTS OF DIVORCE ON CHILDREN

This is Jared's story of being part of a blended family, of the lessons he learned, and of the things he had to deal with as the result of being from a broken home.

Jared Shares His Story

Where do I even begin? With a mom, stepdad, stepmom, dad, two stepsiblings, one blood sibling, and two adopted siblings, it is a question I often ponder when people ask me about my family. That does not include the endless number of extended family members, many of whom I have close relationships with, as well. It is hard to shrink 33 years of life into a few paragraphs, but I will give it my best shot.

I am not sure if there is any scientific proof, but I would bet that many readers of this book who are a product of divorced parents will agree with me: being a child of divorced parents changes your outlook on life. In my case, I was not even old enough to remember life before my parents divorced and my mother married Joe. I was a baby at the time of the divorce and was only 2 years old when my mom remarried.

I do not think about it too much now or wish things had been different in any way, but my younger self always wondered if, somehow, I was the reason for the divorce. Perhaps I wasn't good enough. I felt responsible for my father and mother divorcing, even though I was only 6 months old when they separated. Writing my story helped me to understand how children think and how divorce can affect them.

As I have grown older and more aware of the circumstances, I know that such fears are untrue. I recall back in college when someone asked me what my greatest fear was. My answer remains true today as a married man: it is getting divorced.

On the other hand, there are many positives to being a product of divorced parents. My stepdad, Joe, and my stepsiblings joined the party when I was 2. I spent most of my time between the ages of 2 and 7 getting acquainted with the new family members and bonding with my mom, brother, and grandma. The consistency, the love, and the stability of my home was a huge part of my life that helped mold me. As previously mentioned, my grandma loved me as much as possible. I had just turned 8 when she passed away in 1997.

Shortly after, we adopted the first of two children into our family. The last child in the family was adopted several years later and will be (hopefully) leaving the nest in four years, so Mom and Joe can enjoy their retirement years. It is wild to think that Mom and Joe have had kids in their house (since their marriage) for 31 years and counting, and I originally planned to be the last one out of the house 15 years ago.

When I was in middle school and high school, my parents worked more than they were at home in order to support our family. I spent most of my time after school hanging out with friends in the neighborhood and competing in sporting events that my parents tried their best to attend. When I was old enough to drive, I worked and spent time with friends when not at school. That led to an easy decision to attend my dream school six hours from home – the University of Tennessee in Knoxville.

Being a product of a blended family is not easy by any means, but it provides growth opportunities within the family structure that I am not sure exist in "normal" families. Building relationships with my siblings, their spouses and their children has been a wonderful experience that would not have been possible without the blended structure of our family. We continue to function as a unit and still get together for family vacations and holidays, as well as the typical trips I make back to my hometown. I would not trade the experience of growing up in a large, blended family for anything. It helped me develop the stability and emotional intelligence I use today.

My early years of life I was not close to my dad, however, I did finally form a relationship with him as I grew older, and I would visit him quite often when I came home from college. Thankfully, we have gotten closer to each other over the years.

LESSONS AT A GLANCE

* Children, no matter the age, can feel responsible for divorce, as if they did something wrong or were not good enough.

* Being a child of divorced parents affects people and may cause them to be afraid of being "set up" for divorce as adults.

* Consistency, love, and stability in the home can be a factor to break the cycle for the children and help relationships to heal.

* There can also be benefits and opportunities that come with a large, blended family.

YOUR NEXT STEPS

1. Pay attention for any signs that the children feel responsible for the divorce. It can make them afraid of relationships if the core issue is not resolved. Make sure they know and understand that they are not to blame. Bring in a counselor or therapist, if needed.

2. Emotional healing must be a priority when anyone is wounded in relationships. Get the healing needed.

3. Pour love into all the children and help establish emotional stability while they are still in the home.

CHAPTER 12

NEVER BIGGER THAN YOUR PARENTS

Sometimes, as you are adjusting to the blend, there can be a big shift in your original plans. Life changes. Lori never lived with us full time. She always stayed with her mother, but she came over often on weekends. She played softball and was an extremely competitive player. We watched her games as often as we could in between running after the other children.

She had to grow up way too fast. Lori was almost 16 when Zach was born and was too young to care for him by herself. Joe and I had only been married four years at the time. This was another transitional phrase we – as well as Lori – were to go through. She moved in with us so she could continue her education and lived with us for less than a year. Zach was in daycare during the day. He was in Lori's room with her at night. However, we monitored him to make sure he was taken care of.

When Zach was 9 months old, my mom was diagnosed with ALS (Lou Gehrig's Disease.) She moved in with us so we could take care of her. Lori and Zach (who was 1 by this time) then moved back to her mother's house until my mother passed away.

When Zach was 18 months old, Lori brought him to stay with us permanently. She did not stay. We adopted Zach. Lori then withdrew from Joe and the family for years. I am sure having a child at such an early age was a factor in that. We have always tried to show Lori support; it was she who pulled away from us. Life situations have a way of doing that to family members. We must strive to always remain family through it all. Thankfully over the years she has become closer to the family. Zach always knew he was adopted. He was such a loving child; however, he had insecurities he had to deal with, and we have often wondered if it was from being born to such a young mother.

Joe and I both worked the night shift at Goodyear, and Zach did not want us to leave at night. Going out the door broke my heart several times. Zach would stay up and run after us, crying that we were leaving him. I decided to quit working at Goodyear when he was 3 to try to make him feel more secure and to help him realize we were there for him. My working night shift was hard on the children and on me. I purchased an existing daycare so that Zach was with me not only at night, but also during the day.

Along every step of our journey, we tried to focus on what was best for our children. We cannot imagine not having Zach in our lives. He has always been a delightful child and has brought us so much joy. From the very beginning, I fell in love with Zach and his "big loving heart." As they were growing up, I always told my boys, "You will never be bigger than me, no matter how big or tall you get." A funny story: When Zach was about 13 years old, he was quite a bit larger than me. He was not listening to me over something I was telling him to do. He took off running away from me, which infuriated me at the time. I swooped up a rock to get his attention. I knew I was not going to hit him, but I threw it so he would see it and stop. He stopped, turned, and stared at me. I said, "You had better come to me now." It got his attention. He came back, and he realized at that point that no matter how big you get, you will never get "bigger than your parents." He is now 6 feet 4 inches tall, but my 5-foot-6 frame is "bigger" than his, and always will be. Zach never ran from me again.

Establish this with your children. Respect is the key. You must get your bluff in on the children, or they will get the bluff on you. Who is going to conquer?

I wanted my children to be mine for life. I wanted them to know I would always be present for them, I would love them, and I would not tolerate being disrespected in any way. Joe and I demanded respect as their parents, and we respected each child on each level as they grew. They knew their boundaries and respected them.

When adopting, you are accepting a child from a person who cannot take care of their little one's well-being. You then become the parent to that child and help them to grow and to be productive. Our goal was to teach all our children to flourish in all their ways and to learn to be dependent upon their Heavenly Father.

Zach has grown into a wonderful man and an overall great person. His devotion to us never ceases to amaze me. He has such a huge heart, which I refer to as the size of Texas. He recently started singing in church, and I am so proud of him.

After six years of dating, Zach finally talked Adyee into marrying him. She was slower than I was when Joe was persistent in marrying me. She is a precious daughter-in-law whom we have welcomed with open arms. Another win. Two grandsons were added to our family. Zach and his wife have two sons who love their grandparents. We are truly blessed. If I had only known, when I was told I would not have children, the plans God had for me. Wow!

LESSONS AT A GLANCE

- Sometimes circumstances in life change our paths unexpectedly, but we can adapt and grow from it.
- Children can have insecurities that make things challenging, but with extra care and understanding, they can work through them.
- It is always most important to do what is, overall, best for the children.
- Your children will never be "bigger than you." Respect is the key.

YOUR NEXT STEPS

1. Pay close attention to whether your child displays insecurities so you can help them work through it at the time, rather than waiting. Over time, the insecurities only grow stronger.

2. Children should be the focus. I have always said, and will continue to say, that in a blended family, the children must be the focus. They have experienced losses, as well, and need to recoup.

3. Let the children know they will never be bigger than you. Get your bluff in on them or they will bluff you later in life. Enforce respect.

4. We all want to raise well-balanced productive children. The key is to teach them about our Heavenly Father. Then neither you nor the children will ever lack anything. Matthew 6:33 says: "But seek ye first the kingdom of God, and His righteousness; and all these things will be added unto you."

CHAPTER 13

LEARNING, GROWING, AND SHARING

This is Zach's story told from his perspective of being adopted and becoming part of a blended family. He told us that writing his story gave him a deeper appreciation for his adoption journey. Notice the lessons Zach learned and the way he has grown from what he learned. He has plans to share those learnings. This is priceless.

Zach Shares His Adoption Journey

My experience with a blended family is a blessing, to say the least. My biological mother was 15 when she became pregnant with me. She was not in the place to take care of me at the time I was born. I commend her for making the choice by letting my parents adopt me. I have a respect and love for her for making the choice of what was best for me at her immature age. I feel I have more understanding and empathy for others because I recognize the choices she could have made.

I was then not only blessed with two amazing parents, but also with three brothers. I cannot imagine my life any different.

Writing this chapter opened my eyes to the things that really matter to me, and that is God, family, choices, memories, and I must add traveling/experiences. Traveling was important to my parents, and we went to a lot of cool places as I was growing up, including Colorado, Montana, Yellowstone, Branson, and Mexico, just to name a few. I want to say thank you to my parents for the awesome experiences. I had an awesome childhood.

I could not have asked for better examples of what parents should be. My dad taught me everything I know mechanically, and he worked hard in everything he did. My mom taught me how to seek God, how to love with all your heart, and how not to run from her (or I would get a rock thrown to get my attention). She also taught me if I did not behave in church, I would get a spanking (which happened often). Being required to go to church was something I didn't understand as a child. Now that I'm grown up and have children, I can look back and understand the changes it has made in my life. There were invaluable lessons, to say the least.

My parents hosted all the holidays and special events for our family; therefore, I grew up having a relationship with all my cousins and relatives. I have seen a lot of family members pass away over the years, which taught me to enjoy the moments. My parents taught me selfless love by example. They not only talked about it, but they showed it in all their actions.

My brothers helped mold me into who I am today. Fast forward: Lori had my little brothers, Ben and Alijah. Ben was adopted by a family that is close to us, and we have a good relationship and get to visit quite often. I even lived with Ben and his parents after I graduated from high school for a while. Alijah was also adopted by my parents.

All I can say is, time flies. I admit I made some bad choices I should not have made. Thankfully, my parents were praying for me, and God had His hand on me. Now it is like I blinked, and my brothers have families of their own. Ben and Alijah are teenagers, and I am 27 and married to my beautiful wife. We have a 6-year-old son and a 10-month-old son. I hope my parents are around for years to come to enjoy their grandchildren. I am thankful I get to teach my children the valuable lessons they taught me.

Writing my story opened my eyes to how blessed I truly am. I am thankful to have my parents (Joe and May), who poured nothing but love into me. The connection I have to all my brothers is a Godsend. I was taught the love of God and having that instilled in me changed the course of my life.

I will be sharing my stories with my children and my younger brothers about the hard knock lessons of life I learned, including peer pressure, drinking, and even trying drugs, so hopefully they will not have to learn the way I did. I am still learning and growing, but as I do, I will share the truths I learn with others.

LESSONS AT A GLANCE

❉ Sometimes it can take years to truly understand what matters most to you.

❉ Family plays such an important role in the journey.

❉ Even when we make unfavorable choices, God has His hand on us the whole time.

❉ Time passes quickly and before you know it, you are handing your childhood lessons down to your own children.

YOUR NEXT STEPS

1. Recognize some of the choices you and others have made. See where you can show compassion, love, and understanding. Extend grace, whether it is to others or to yourself.

2. Write down what is truly most important to you. Think about or write about why these things are so important. Allow yourself to really feel it.

3. Realize that, from time to time, we all will make a choice we regret. If we have had good values instilled, if we pray, and if we are led by our Creator, we will always make better choices. What steps are you taking to make better choices?

4. Think about the lessons you have learned over your life that you can pass on to your family. The hard knock lessons of life can open the eyes of others when we are willing to share them.

CHAPTER 14

ADOPTION JOURNEY

When Lori was 28, she had another baby and was not in a place where she could care for him. His name was Ben. Out of love for the child, everyone involved felt it best to adopt him out. At the time that Ben was born we were deeply involved at the restaurant we owned. You could say we were married to it, as anyone who has ever owned such a business can understand. Restaurant work is something we thought we would enjoy, but it did not take long to realize it was not what we were meant to do. It was long hours and too much demanding work and very little pay. The gift of adoption can be a blessing for so many. Next is the heartfelt story of a mother who was trusting, and it worked out for the best.

Joe had retired from Goodyear after 33 years of service. The first couple of years we catered to the Goodyear plant three shifts a day, and we loved it. Since we had both worked there for years, it was like taking food to family. However, two years into the business, Joe was asked to build them their own cafeteria, and we stopped catering. At that point, Joe was ready to get out of the restaurant business. We did not know what our future held, but we knew it was not a restaurant.

During this restaurant-running season of our life, Ben was adopted by a couple we had known for years who could not have children. He taught us a lesson on bonding with children that amazes us to this day.

Ben was cared for by Nana, his maternal grandmother, and her husband Kenny. Kenny was hands on 24/7 with Ben as Nana worked full time. When Ben was 5 months old the adoptive parents were allowed to take him home with them. Our agreement was we would all still be involved in his life.

We celebrated his 1st and his 2nd birthday together with them and Christmas in their home. When he was 2 years old, they brought him for a visit. On the way, he started saying, "Granddaddy Kenny." His adoptive mother Leilani was amazed at how elated he was to get to see Grandad, who had been his primary caregiver for the first five months of his life. The bond had formed at the start of his life, and it was real. This was the first time the bond was so evident. To this day, (he just turned 15) when he comes to visit, he still prefers to stay with Grandaddy Kenny and Nana. Ben has a huge heart and is aware how much his brothers, Zach and Alijah, and his family love him. We see him often and are so glad that not only the boys, but all the grandparents, are in Ben's life.

Had we known that 13 months later Alijah would be born, we would have kept Ben. We had no clue, of course. However, I do believe he is where he is meant to be, with parents he was meant to be with. We have committed Ben to the Lord, and we know he shall be established. "Commit to the Lord whatever you do, and He will establish your plans" (Proverbs 16:3).

Ben's adoptive mother Leilani Harvey tells the adoption story through her eyes, as a woman who had felt such hopelessness, her heart shattered with wanting to be a mother. She tried to hold on to the dream, and then did the only thing she knew to do: she turned it over to her Creator. She then got the baby she believed God for.

Recently we had a conversation with Ben about how Zach and Alijah were adopted by us, and we know in our hearts Ben was meant to be with Leilani. Ben said, "I cannot imagine my life being any different." A beautiful story unfolds here.

Leilani's Shares

My journey with Ben started long ago. I always wanted one thing in life, which was to be a mother. When I was in my late teens, I found out that I would not be able to physically have children. I was heartbroken. I prayed and prayed, and yet for every positive step I took forward, I would take two steps back.

After years of heartbreak trying to conceive, I gave up and decided to let go of my dream. If God meant for me to be a mother, then he would make a way. I turned it over to Him.

In October 2008 my best friend contacted me, asking if I wanted a baby. I was shocked! Ben was 5 months old at the time. I spoke with my spouse, and we agreed to visit Ben's grandparents, who were raising him. We went to West Tennessee the following weekend.

To say that I fell in love is an understatement! He was beautiful! He was healthy, happy, and always smiling and laughing. We immediately felt a connection with Ben. We stayed the weekend to see how things would go.

On Sunday afternoon, his grandparents asked if we wanted to adopt him. There are no words to express how my world felt complete for the very first time. I felt like all that I had been through in life, God was blessing me in the highest honor by allowing me to be Ben's mom.

After that weekend, once home, we started the adoption process and retained an attorney in West Tennessee. We met with an adoption agency in Nashville and were assigned an amazing case worker. She answered all the questions we had and collaborated with us on everything.

That Thanksgiving, my best friend brought Ben to us to spend the week. The weekend after we took him back to his grandparents, they had his things loaded and sent him back home with us.

Less than a month later, our case worker contacted me and said that everything had gone through. We were legally able to adopt Ben. It was the best Christmas gift I ever received. I was not sure what I had done in my life that God entrusted me to be Ben's mom, but I was grateful and thankful for this amazing blessing.

On June 15, 2009, we went to court, and we became legal parents to Ben. When I received his "new" birth certificate in the mail, and it showed my name as the birth mother, my life came full circle. Being Ben's mother is the greatest blessing. I am so thankful that God would entrust me with something/someone so precious. I went from having a heavy, broken heart to a complete, wide-open heart.

We stay connected and visit all his grandparents in West Tennessee and Kentucky; they are blessings to Ben and us. We may not see each other as much since he is older, but there is still communication and appreciation for all of them. Ben also stays in touch with his brothers.

We were not sure about telling him he was adopted; however, we were asked to always be truthful with him if he brought it up. We waited until he approached us, out of fear he would be hurt. Ben knew from the beginning he had brothers, and it was he who approached and asked how they were his brothers. He had an idea he was adopted; he just was not sure.

In a non-emotional state, we explained he was adopted and, at first, he did not believe us. We had to show him his birth certificate and the adoption papers for him to believe it. He had no hang-ups on it. I had wrestled with how to tell him for a long time. It worked out perfectly, just like it should have.

Ben is 15 now. He is kind, generous, a good human, and a typical teenager. He is beautiful, sweet, kind, funny, positive, and an exceptionally good boy. He also has a heart for others. He has been my biggest supporter, and we pull each other out of our own life issues all the time.

His dad and I divorced a few years ago. Ben has stayed close to his dad, however. I do wonder if our Creator gave us Ben to pull us through the roughest storms of our life. Ben keeps me going daily. I am so proud of the man he is becoming, as he has been through a lot of changes in the last three years. He has kept his head held high, walked me through my new journey, (another story for another time), and continued to support me and be my rock.

I could not ask for a better son; he is my everything. The reward of the adoption journey is more than I could ever have imagined, and I cannot possibly envision my life without Ben in it.

I could not have figured out this adoption on my own. I did not have the understanding. I thank God for directing my path, making a way where there was no way, and giving me Ben. "Trust in the Lord with all thine heart; and lean not unto thine own understanding. In all thy ways acknowledge him, and he shall direct thy paths" (Prov. 3:5-6).

My journey has continued. I became a foster mother. God is continuing to bless me, and my broken heart is far from me. I always wanted children and now I am blessed to nurture many children. I thought I would never have children in my life, but I now have a steady supply. Only God! [1] (See a letter from a foster mom in the companion workbook.)

LESSONS AT A GLANCE

✽ If you are heartbroken over not being able to have children, remember there are other ways. Turn it over to God.

✽ There are numerous necessary steps to adoption, but it is worth the journey.

✽ It is important always to tell the truth – keeping emotions out of the discussion. Honesty with the children is key to a loving connection.

✽ Adoption is a huge honor. The bond can become just as real as it would be with biological parents.

YOUR NEXT STEPS

1. If it is in your heart to become a parent, research your options. Prayers can be answered in unexpected ways.

2. Do not be afraid to tell children the truth; they may already know it deep inside. Be prepared for what you will say and how you will communicate when the time comes.

3. When faced with resistance, keep the course until you win. Do the steps it takes.

4. Write down your dreams and keep them at the forefront of your mind. You never know how it will happen. Keep it alive and it can come true. Know that the "how" is not ours to figure out. Thank God for making a path for you when you cannot see one.

CHAPTER 15

TRUTH RULES

When Lori was 29, she had another baby, named Alijah. She was not at a place to care for him, so we brought him home with us from the hospital. We did not have plans for another child, but as you know, plans can change.

Joe had no intention of keeping Alijah; however, we fell in love, and we were in a place where we could adopt him. We were blessed to be able to add him as another son to our blend. All three children – Zach, Ben, and Alijah – knew Lori had given birth to them but, due to her circumstances and for their well-being, she loved them enough to let someone else raise them. I commend her for that.

Alijah is bi-racial and even though he and Ben are biological brothers, Alijah is a lot darker than Ben. He was 4 when he first noticed a difference in his color. He came in from daycare with a puzzled look and said, "Me and my friend Chloe are darker than everyone else. Why?" Alijah asked why he was different, and with no emotions involved, we explained his parents to him. We also told him we were his adoptive parents. We showed him a picture of Lori and his biological dad and explained that is how he got his color.

Children are very inquisitive and when given the truth versus a lie – or a half-truth or a made-up story – they can accept the truth. If they find out later a lie was told, it can do more damage. When telling the truth, you never have to back track, cover up, and invent a lie to cover a lie.

When deep feelings are present and they are presented in a negative way, stored emotions can result. Stored emotions can have negative effects throughout a person's life. This can cause damage to an individual unless the emotions are dealt with. No such emotions were present when we explained Alijah's story to him, and he simply said "OK" and took off playing.

He has never had any hang-ups with his color. He knows he is loved, and he is supported. He is such a well-rounded young man. He is good-natured and has a laid-back attitude far beyond his years. He has a calmness about him, much like Joe. I remind him quite often that he is "our baby."

Recently at a school recognition program, someone behind us in the crowd announced they were the oldest parents there. I chimed in with a laugh and said, "No, we are the oldest parents!" I asked Alijah, "Does that bother you?" His reply was another moment that will always be etched in my mind. With a sincere, loving look he said, "You may be the oldest, but you are the very best parents ever, in my book." As you see he is also a smooth talker, and he has our hearts.

After having had four miscarriages, these boys are gifts, and they are a reminder to me: "God Is faithful" (Hebrews 10:23).

Adoption Through Alijah's Eyes

Alijah was 12 years old at the time he wrote his perspective on being adopted. Notice how much wisdom can come from children, even at an early age.

I can say adoption can be a blessing, or at least for me it has been. I would not have had a dad if I had not been adopted. I have never seen my biological dad. He saw me when I was born, but since I have gotten older, he has never called or reached out to me. I am OK with it. You do not know people unless you spend time with them. I would not know him anyway.

I am close to all my brothers. The relationship we have would not have been as strong as it is now if I had not been adopted by my parents. I am the youngest child, and even though my parents are older, they have done a lot of things with me. I cannot imagine my life any different. However, if I had not been adopted, I know my life would have a totally different look. It would not be like it is now, for sure.

I do see my biological mother every so often; I still consider her as my mother, and I am thankful she had me. I know I have siblings from my biological dad that I have never seen, and sometimes that bothers me. I figure one day, if it is meant to be, we will connect. I will continue my life, trusting I am where I am meant to be, with parents that love me and support me.

LESSONS AT A GLANCE

❋ Stored emotions can affect a child throughout their life. Being honest in a non-emotional way can help them process the truth, without attaching negative emotions.

❋ Adoption can be a blessing.

❋ Even at a young age, children have much wisdom regarding their situations, their surroundings, and the love they receive.

YOUR NEXT STEPS

1. Make it a point to show your children love and treat them equally, no matter what. Despite any differences or unique ways, they may have. They became yours with flaws, behaviors, and maybe learned behaviors from others. However, love can prevail over it all.

2. If you have a bi-racial, an adopted child, or a stepchild treat them with respect, always remembering that they are no different than you are.

3. Always tell the truth. Listen for the truth or a half-truth and always correct the truth when you identify it. This could keep your child from falling for a lie later in life.

4. Talk to the children in positive affirmations to secure the child. Let go of all emotions when dealing with questions from your children. Answer in nonjudgmental tones of voice and body language, children know when you don't.

CHAPTER 16

ADOPTION AND ACCEPTANCE

Sometimes the children or families involved in a private adoption wish to reach the birth parents. The levels of acceptance can vary when doing so, as can the range of emotions. Next are some adoption stories from others that have touched my heart.

A Story from D.C., a Friend from CA Shares

I was an adopted child, and I do not remember a time when I did not know it. My mom always made it clear that I was wanted and loved. She explained my birth mother was young and she just wanted the best for me. I never felt like something was missing in my life. I was content with not searching for my birth mother. It was my mom who wanted me to find my birth mother, just so she could thank her. My adoption was a private adoption, so all I had was a signed legal document that had my birth mother's and my grandfather's signatures on it. So, I had names.

Occasionally, my mom would ask me to search for my birth mother. One day, I found a post on a message board that a woman was looking for the daughter she gave up on my birthdate, and at the same hospital where I was born. The clincher was, she was looking for my name, she just had it misspelled. I timidly called the number and a couple of hours later she called me back and we had a great reunion over the phone.

I was traveling close to where she lived a few weeks later and we made plans to meet. She and her husband came to meet me and my husband. It was a nice meeting. We talked about everything we could. I discovered I have two half-brothers that I look exactly like. We talked about my family, how my life was growing up, and the entire situation around her pregnancy and my subsequent adoption.

I was sad to hear how she had been treated by her mother over the pregnancy. It was back in the 1970s and she had been hidden for months prior to my birth. She had just turned 16 and was not allowed to see me after I was born.

We made plans for her to come and meet my children and my parents. The visit with my kids went great, and we enjoyed having her in our home. However, the visit with my birth mother was not good; my mother got terribly upset, agitated, and rude the entire time we were there, even though she had told me for 30 years that she just wanted to thank my birth mother for having me. I assume fear stepped in, and my mom worried that now that I'd met my birth mother, I would forget the mom who raised me. At that time, my birth mother and I decided it clearly upset my mom and we would have to stay connected privately. It made me sad, but we both agreed.

The next year, I was traveling through their town, so she and her husband invited me to come to their home and meet my two half-brothers. They were concerned and told me that the boys may not be very receptive. Overall, it was a nice visit, but I got the impression that they were not interested in having me be a part of the family. We talked about the situation and this time it was me who said, "I ought to step back and stay out of the way, since it clearly upset them."

It made me sad, however, again we both agreed. Now, my birth mom and I are just friends on Facebook. We do not connect, call, or reach out at all. Neither one wants to interfere or cause problems for each other, but I know that if I needed her, she would be there.

Another Private Adoption Story

An 80-year-old acquaintance I recently met was talking to me about her adoption. Her adopted mother always told her she was adopted; the adoption agency told her not to keep that from her, or she would feel her life had been a lie. She tried on several occasions to find her birth parents.

In 1940, her adoption was a closed adoption, and she could not get any leads. One of her friends, a few years ago, gifted her with Ancestory.com; she found a sister, a few nieces, and a cousin. She was received by some of her original family immediately; however, one cousin was very skeptical until she talked with the others.

She knew she could not push herself on any of the family members; they did not know her. She connects with a lot of her family through Facebook. She said it surprised her how much she looks like her siblings. What was amazing to her was, after a lifetime, she was able to connect and was received as family.

LESSONS AT A GLANCE

✳ Meeting birth parents/family can be an emotional experience for all parties involved.

✳ The level of acceptance by family members can vary.

✳ Careful consideration must be made before deciding to search for or meet the biological family.

YOUR NEXT STEPS

1. If you are in a private adoption, make sure you are not pushing yourself or your children on people.

2. Give thought to whether you are certain you want to find relatives. Be cautious and understand that you may not be welcomed by everyone.

CHAPTER 17

PAIN CAN CAUSE CHANGE

Gerald was not paying child support for the boys after our divorce. I understood that sometimes the pain of losing a family can cause a person not to pay child support, especially if they did not want a divorce. I was not about to force him to pay and never talked badly about him to the children.

However, one day at church our pastor said, "If you owe child support then you need to pay it, it validates the children, and they know they were wanted." I had never looked at it that way. The pastor also said, "If you are supposed to get child support, get it. It validates the children." The boys were 13 and 16 at this time. I called the boys' dad over and told him how they wanted to know what happened that caused us to divorce. I explained how we were so far apart in our values and our vision, that our marriage did not work. I then told him I was going for child support. It was a large amount of money he owed.

Throughout all the phases of life, the changes, and the adjustments, one thing we learned was that pain can cause change. Pain brings awareness to the situation and ultimately will expose the truth, which is what brings the transformation needed.

When we went to court, the child support lady called me out: "Mrs. Simpson, we need to work this out, to keep this from going before the judge." I replied, "No, Ma'am. We have been here several times, and nothing changes." She responded, "Mrs. Simpson, some men pay child support and some men do not. Apparently, you have one that does not." I answered, "I want to see the judge. Apparently, we have not made the pain great enough."

The judge told Gerald to pay it off, however long it took He put the fear in him either to pay or to go to jail. He paid. Jonathan was 19 when Gerald stopped paying and Jared was 23. I had to knock off a year when I realized Jonathan was 19. I called my ex-husband and told him that he overpaid. He responded with, "I am not going back before the judge."

Pain caused the change. Money, such as child support, can cause money blocks with children later in life if not dealt with head on. We must figure out what pain we need in order to change our lives. If other behavior changes need to happen for our children or other family members, we must figure out a form of pain to get the results we want.

Gerald paid the child support, and that paid off for everyone. It had a domino effect; a deeper bond with the boys was formed, and they felt worth from him. They knew he loved them, and he supported them in their life's journey. I finally understood what the pastor meant when she made that statement in church that day. Child support validates your children.

Teaching Children Responsibility

Another painful moment we experienced as the children got older was learning we had to make the children responsible. Joe gave the two oldest children – Chris and Lori – cars when they turned 16. He had always told them he would, and he kept his word. They did not have to pay for anything. He wanted more for them than he had growing up, so we paid for their cars, their insurance and even helped them with gas.

The pain caused a change. Joe was still paying child support for Lori at this time; I was not getting child support at this time. In addition to this added expense, we were also taking care of my mother, his dad, and my brother simultaneously. This led us to have to file for bankruptcy. That was an embarrassment and a very discouraging and trying time for us. Some things you learn the hard way, and this was an extremely hard lesson.

We made the next two children – Jonathan and Jared – pay for their own cars and their insurance. We gave them gas money. They learned responsibility early on. Today, the older two still struggle with responsibility.

Make kids responsible or they will struggle later, and it can take years for them to learn accountability on their own. We wish this was something we had known before making this mistake, so now we want to let as many as we can know the lesson, we learned the hard way.

Spoiling children, as we have learned, does not mean giving them everything in monetary ways. It means to spoil them with your love, and they will remain your children forever.

LESSONS AT A GLANCE

❋ Pain has a way of causing change. When the pain is great enough, people are likely to make the change regarding bad choices, unhealthy lifestyles, or whatever it is where change is needed.

❋ Pain will bring awareness to the situation. Once awareness is made the truth can be exposed to bring the transformation needed.

❋ Child support validates the children. It is important to receive and pay child support.

❋ Receiving child support can help prevent the children from money blocks later in life.

❋ Teach children responsibility early on to help them along their journey.

YOUR NEXT STEPS

1. Notice what changes are necessary.

2. Look at how implementing those changes can be beneficial to the children and the family as a whole.

3. Set a plan in place to cause the change, whether it is for you as the parent or for the children.

4. If stuck in unhealthy pain, figure out where it is from and find a way to change and get rid of it. This is another area where counselors, therapists, or even pastors can help find your answers.

CHAPTER 18

BEHIND THE SCENES

A family unit can be strong, and no one would know they were a blended family or that they had any struggles in blending. However, there is always a "behind the scenes" story. Other blended families share their journeys, their successes, and the lessons they learned.

Brad and Cindi Cook's Blended Family Story

At the time of the interview in 2021, Brad and Cindi Cook had been married 13 years and together for 15. They were both divorced. They dated for a year and a half before making the commitment to marriage. They respected each other and their individual children. What worked for them was spending time with their own children, both individually and as a family. Each parent spent time with each other's children, as well, to build trust with all of them.

Cindi said, "The children are not who falls in love, it is the parents. Children's love must be allowed to grow as the family unit comes together." It took cultivating relationships with each child for them to be able to adjust. Cindi and her children not only had to adjust to a new marriage, but also to new surroundings, since she moved them all to another city.

When they married, Cindi's had two daughters Libby (7) and Molly (11). Brad's had a son Cace (9) and a daughter Chloe (7). Molly was going into the seventh grade, and the merger was very hard. The struggles were real, with jealousy probably the hardest to deal with. As mothers, we want to treat all the children the same; however, when we do that, our own children feel left out. If one girl goes shopping, they all feel like they need to go shopping.

If the other parents are involved, we must deal with that, as well. Trying to balance this is not an easy task, especially while trying to respect the children's space and work with both sets of parents, our own roles, and the roles of our spouses. The Cooks say it took a long time for the girls to let Brad do errands for them that they felt like their mom could manage. The same was true for Brad's children. It took a while for them to adjust to Cindi's stepping in and helping. Having children so close in age was hard. There was a lot of competition because of that. Brad and Cindi knew they could not get to the point of giving in or giving up. Time would be their biggest friend. They kept their communication open with each other and never took anything that the children said or did personally.

It was extremely hard for Cindi. After moving to another city, she had no support system, and she did not even have any divorced friends with whom she could bounce off the things she was encountering. One thing to her advantage was her degree in counseling. She said she knew that when you step back, you can see more clearly. She saw through the eyes of the children and stepped into their shoes, always trying to see where they were coming from. She did not have all the answers, but she could point to sources where answers could be found. She also had her faith.

Cindi had no plans to be a divorcee, and she struggled with the break in her marriage. She was not about to go through a divorce again. That was one of the things that helped her along the journey. Love was also a big factor. She and Brad adored each other. They treated each other as king and queen, and they wanted to be a helper to each other's children, not just focusing on their own gain. They held the same values and visions and wanted the same things in life. They were best friends. They both held a balance with the exes and included each other in all decisions.

Cace was the youngest, and he and Cindi bonded right away. Brad and Cindi were always there to support all the children, regardless of what they were into. The children all excelled and were successful. Brad and Cindi believed that the most important thing to express to the children is that they had nothing to do with their parents' marriages ending. Cindi said she is so thankful for Brad; he poured his love into her, into her girls, and into their blended family. "The blend was hard and challenging, but so worth it," she said.

The Blend Through Kristen Cole's Eyes

Kristen Cole also worked at the Aloha Pools store. This is her take on the blend. As a kid, I felt like I did not belong in some places, that I was 'just the stepchild' and not the actual child. I never liked being introduced as someone else's child, rather than 'our child.' It took a toll on me emotionally. The older I got, the less I would let it get to me. I felt left out but tried to blend as much as I could with the family. The blend provided me with a total of four sisters (two biological, one half, one stepsister) and one stepbrother. I am now close to all of them.

With the blend, I got to spend truly little time with my dad. I only went to his house twice a month. I wish we had had more time together, but, unfortunately, it was not possible. He was in a blended family, as well.

At 18, I had to have open heart surgery. I was surrounded by everyone on both sides of my family. They were there every step of the way. That was the first time since I was probably 4 that both my mom and dad were in the same room together with just me. No matter how old you are, you still want to have both parents in your life and (you want to) know that you are important to them. They all came together during this demanding situation and put their differences aside. I am forever grateful.

My biggest takeaway from the blend was the added support from having an additional family. My step-grandparents have been so good to me. Having additional family members has been beneficial in times of loss and in times of celebration. I know I will always have family that supports me, no matter what I do or where I go. Life in the blend was tough, I admit. However, we are all survivors and much stronger because of it.

"Our" Children

I had a coaching client tell me that when she got married, she had one daughter, he had one daughter and they had one daughter together. For years, they introduced the kids as "his, hers, and ours." When the youngest was 7, the girls told the adults they did not like being called "his, hers, and ours." They said they were all sisters. I encourage you to try to make your blend focus on "ours." It is not the children's fault when divorce happens, and they deserve to feel loved equally.

A Grandparent's Story

One grandparent set aside money for his grandchildren's college; however, after a divorce, the grandchildren did not even recognize him as their grandparent.

Remember that it is not the fault of the grandparents, the children, or others who have grown to love the children when a marriage ends, yet many of them get wounded when families split.

Letting Go

Another friend, who had two children, told me he married a woman who had two children, which he adopted. They had been married for eight years when the wife decided she wanted to go back to school. My friend thought everything was good, but he came back from a business trip, and his wife had moved out. He was floored.

He said, "It is impossible to live with someone that is not content. You cannot control their behavior, nor another person's actions." A personal empowerment coach once said to me, "If you did not create it, you did not cause it, and you have no control over it; You must let it go."

Feeling an Outcast

Amber, a friend of mine, was in a blended family of 10 children. She said her life resembled "a stiff family environment that was not a good place to be."

Her dad never went against her stepmother, and sometimes she was wrong. Years later, after her dad passed away, the stepmother apologized to the children and admitted she had been wrong many times.

What helped Amber the most was knowing her dad loved her. She said the best advice she could give is that parents should always get along in a blended family and be aware of the family environment. Amber was treated as an outcast by the other stepchildren, and she said the parents need to be present and aware of each child equally to prevent them from feeling as she did, like an outcast in her own home.

Stay On The Same Page

While coaching another client, Lisa with a blended family of eight children, her advice was to stay on the same page with parenting. She had four children and he had three children who lived in their home all the time. He had a daughter who lived out of state with her mother. None of the children in the home had the other parents available to them; the "blended" parents were all the children had.

The biggest challenge they had to work through was the different parenting styles. He had a way of parenting, and she had a way of parenting. The children played on that. Resentments and offenses happened because of the imbalance. She said, "With seven children, all of them are different and not all of them will like each other, and that is OK." Having seven children full-time growing up was hard, always running in all different directions with sports, school activities, etc.

The vacations to the lake and holidays with those seven children were off the charts. They turned heads everywhere they went; people would stare. She felt like they were a parade; her husband would lead, the children would occupy the middle, and she would act as the caboose, keeping everyone in line. She says she considered the possibility of throwing candy to the onlookers, but instead, she just smiled and waved. When asked, both parents always answered, "Yes, they are all ours."

She knows that one day, when she and her husband are on the lake fishing and reflecting on their lives and on their children's lives, they will say, "It was hard. It was a challenge, but the children made it and we did, too." They are thankful for their blended journey, and they know God has a plan and they will continue to trust Him.

LESSONS AT A GLANCE

❊ Just because you fell in love with someone does not mean the children automatically will. They must be allowed time for adjustments and for their love to grow.

❊ Referring to the children as "ours" can help to alleviate jealousy or insecurities.

❊ Others grow to love the children and can get hurt when families split.

❊ It is important for children to be treated equally so they do not feel like outcasts in their own home.

❊ Staying on the same page while parenting is key, whether you have one child in the blend or numerous children.

YOUR NEXT STEPS

1. Spend time with the children individually and as a family unit. Be fully present in these moments to help strengthen the bonds and create memories together.

2. Be patient as you allow the children's love to grow while the family comes together. Recognize that this happens on the child's timetable, not yours, and notice any times you become impatient or have a lack of understanding.

3. Think about what you can do to ensure all children feel included and equally loved.

4. Try to find the balance with all parents involved and discuss how you can stay on the same page for the children's best interests. This can be challenging if animosity is present between any of the parties, but recognize it is for the children's sake and it can keep them from playing you against each other.

CHAPTER 19

BLENDED 52 YEARS

I interviewed Jean and Hayward Laster from Union City, Tennessee. They were married in 1970 and married 52 years as of June 22, 2022, after only knowing each other for six weeks. They are proof that a blended family can survive. I had known Jean and Hayward for many years and was saddened to hear of Hayward's passing not long after the interview. Their remarkable story has been an inspiration to many.

When they married, Hayward had a daughter Tammy (10), a son Timmy (8), and a son Teddy (7). Jean's two boys were Jock (4) and Jai (2). Three years later, they added Rob to the blend. Hayward was a truck driver. Jean worked full-time, as well as being a chauffeur, and managed the household. From the very beginning of the blend, they put strategies in place.

Any time the kids asked to do something or had questions; they would discuss it privately before responding. This stopped the children from playing the parents against each other.

They showed no partiality to any of them; they were all treated the same. The children all came together as a family and soon started recognizing each other as brothers and sisters.

Any time any of the grandparents wanted them, they were allowed to go. They never talked badly about the other parents; they knew children are smart, and they would figure things out on their own.

The children would go back and forth between the other sets of parents. Each had their own set of problems and yet they worked through troubles as any usual family would. They all grew to be well-rounded children.

Hayward and Jean set boundaries, and the children learned what they could cross and what they could not. They were normal children doing normal things. If the children said they would be somewhere, they had better be there, because their parents would check. Jean said, the pain we go through in our own lives must be dealt with to raise children; it is not the children's fault. They said the journey was not easy, but it was so worth it.

Today the children are all thriving in their own lives. Their parents were strong in their faith in God, and they shared that with their children. They said they believed the blend could come together with God, love, and the commitment to stay true to the family unit. They now not only have six children, but they have 13 grandchildren, and their ninth great-grandchild was born before this book was published.

Jean said, "It was truly a ride, but a ride I am so glad I took, for it turned out to be well worth it."

LESSONS AT A GLANCE

✻ The Lasters had strategies in place from the beginning, they stuck to them, and they worked.

✻ Discussing children's questions and requests privately before answering them can keep parents on the same page.

✻ Showing no partiality and refusing to speak badly about the other parents can make for a more peaceful family dynamic.

✻ Setting boundaries and staying true to them is imperative for harmony to exist.

YOUR NEXT STEPS

1. Put strategies and boundaries in place for your family, if you haven't yet. The sooner you do this, the better, as all parties need to learn them and adjust.

2. Discuss your answers before giving an answer to a child to ensure both parents are on the same page.

3. Do not show any partiality. Be cautious in showing favoritism, as children pick up on that quickly.

4. Never talk badly about the other parents.

5. Stay true to God and love each other and the family unit so you can have a successful family with well-balanced children.

CHAPTER 20

TRUSTING THE KEEPER OF THE STARS

Ruth Smith from Colorado shared her story that 24 years ago, when her children were 10 and 8, she moved 100 miles away from their former home and started another life. Life in their previous home had been unpredictable, and she felt they would all be safer if they left. A success story of starting over again; how the blend came together, and two families became one.

They found a way to move, rented a cute house, and made a good team taking on a new community and neighborhood, new schools, and a new job, all while in the company of a young black lab, who was their best friend. A huge, oppressive weight was lifted off their shoulders as they moved in this new direction. Ruth said she returned to her real self, whom she had lost, and she regained her confidence. She also had a peace and calm that she had not felt in years. Notice how she gives credit to God, the Keeper of the Stars, for directing her path.

Eleven months after we had moved to another town, I happened to meet a man named Steve while I was out at a country dance-hall. Trusting the "Keeper of the Stars" certainly was guiding us together; we started dating. Three years later, he proposed. I said, "Yes!"

Four months later, we married. Our children stood up with us at our wedding party. Our friend and pastor sang Tracy Byrd's "Keeper of the Stars" as one of our wedding songs. The lyrics say: "I tip my hat to the Keeper of the Stars. He sure knew what He was doin' when He joined these two hearts."

There were numerous bonus blessings we learned about due to the blend. We learned how to accept people as they are; not to attempt to change others, rather accept them and allow them to be themselves, even if part of it bugs us.

As for the biggest and best bonus, the Lord is with us as our third strand of a strong cord. We are both believers and know God is in our hearts and guiding our marriage. What a difference that makes! Though one may be overpowered, two can defend themselves. "A cord of three strands is not quickly broken" (Eccles. 4:12, New International Version Bible).

What does this all mean? What do we suggest for others? If possible, DON'T divorce. In fact, we have worked with other couples and counseled them to repair, rebuild, and restore their marriages and spare the children the anxiousness and adjustments that come with divorce and later relationships. Sometimes (we get it, we have been there) that is just not an option you can choose, or honestly, that is not one you can easily choose alone. It works only when two people decide together to work to restore their marriage. If you move on/leave a relationship, my prayer is that this chapter and the other chapters in this book will give insights and guidance to help you along your new path.

My husband and I have now been married 20 years and have a loving, supportive relationship. I am incredibly grateful for who he is and that we are together. It is the marriage I dreamed of as a teenager and young adult. However, the early years of our marriage were not without bumps and strains.

Even the most well-adjusted children still struggle with their parents' break-up, let alone as you work to blend and bend to merge into one smoothly functioning home. Through it all, we have learned that we need to connect with our children and truly see and hear them; that was needed when they were in our home as small children, and it is still needed even when they are adults.

We also learned that there is power in prayer, prayer changes things. We can envision things and we can plan, but God already has His ultimate blueprint for everything. We must be open and available to feel His guidance and to jump on board when He calls us to action. We need to continue learning and strengthening our skills and our relationship with Him. His plans will become reality despite our action or inaction. "He telleth the number of the stars; he calleth them all by their names" (Ps. 147:4).

LESSONS AT A GLANCE

- Trust the "Keeper of the Stars."
- The Lord is with us as the third strand of a cord.
- Rather than divorce, making a marriage work is possible if both parties are determined to do so, but only if there is no abuse in the marriage.

YOUR NEXT STEPS

1. Our steps are guided when we trust our Creator.

2. Learn to accept people "as they are." We don't plan to change others; we accept them and allow them to be themselves. Having the Lord with you as the third strand of a strong cord is powerful. You are encouraged to seek Him, trust Him, and let Him be the third strand in your life. "A cord of three strands is not quickly broken" (Ecclesiastes 4:12, NIV).

3. Do not divorce, if that is possible. Get counseling if you loved each other enough to marry at one time. Invest what you must to stay the course. It works best when two people decide together to work to restore their marriage. In some instances, however, it is better to move on, if both aren't invested; or if there is abuse in the marriage.

CHAPTER 21

OVERCOMING GRIEF

Grief is a subject that everyone must walk out on their own journey and on their own time. The overwhelming waves of grief can be a tumultuous journey. As you have read, I have had my share of losses, and I am sure some of you can relate.

Grief comes in many forms, not just death of a loved one. A terminal diagnosis of a loved one can also start the grief process long before the loved one passes. When an animal we love passes, we grieve. I have heard people grieve over a car they loved that was wrecked. Many things can trigger grief.

Divorce can also bring immense grief. Grief in divorce is hard because the person is still alive and often there is no clear understanding of what led to the divorce. However, even if the divorce has not been filed and the couple is unsure of their destination, grief can begin while the partner is still in the home. Children grieve for their parents going through a divorce and, often, long after the divorce.

As I previously mentioned, the divorce along my journey was one of the hardest things I ever went through. I grieved not only that our lives would not continue as a couple, but there was also the grief over losing my dream; my children losing their dad (as a full-time father); losing my parents-in-laws, whom I adored; losing my sisters-in-law; losing the familiar things in my life, the things I had that were "us." It was like my heart was ripped in two. I longed for those things. I hurt over not having my husband touch me when I needed it, to soothe my pain. I was alone and lonely, and the grief was hard to deal with.

I have overcome grief time and again. It is never easy, and it is something you must "go through to get through." [2] The book "Lemons on Friday," written by Mattie Jackson Selecman, is one I highly recommend to anyone grieving. Mattie lost her husband before their first anniversary, and her story explains how she dealt with grief. As I was going through losing a sister, her book was sent to me by one of my sons, and it helped me to get through the process. Understanding and reading about other people's journeys will let us know we are not the only ones going through pain.

Grief is a process, one that only the person grieving can go through. Grief has no respect of age from young to old everyone will experience grief. I know firsthand when I was 10 my dad sold my horse while I was away on a trip, I was overtaken with grief over the loss and of him selling it. I have watched people grieve after retirement over the loss of purpose, drive, friends, and connections. A lot of times they do not pull out of it. Recently a grandmother in our hometown committed suicide because of grief.

No one can speed up the process or help it along. I do recommend talking to a counselor, a coach, a pastor, a therapist – anyone who can relate to grief. Talking can help tremendously. It is also helpful to seek out an inspirational tribe that you can get strength from. No matter what you are going through, others are as well. We need to seek out those who have conquered the things we need to conquer. Seek counsel. "Where no counsel is, the people fall: but in the multitude of counsellors *there is* safety" (Proverbs 11:14).

When we think of our journey and only look at the hard parts of our lives, the hard will become our focus. It can become a drudgery and a challenge that looks impossible to get through. If we look at our journey as it will be supplied for by our Creator, we do not need to know how or what is possible, we only need to know it is possible; our Creator has us and will lead us and guide us for our good.

With that perspective, the journey becomes easier. The gifts begin to show up and the how, the what, and the possible happen. It is true that when we trust, the things needed for the journey will show up.

My first sibling to pass away was from a horrible car accident. My mother seemed to pick up the pieces rather quickly and I did not understand how. I asked, "Mom, how are you doing this? You seem to be coping better than the rest of us." Her response will forever be part of me. "I must remember you." I asked her, "What do you mean?" She said, "I cannot go where Steve is, so I must stay in the present with you, you are my baby." She quoted Luke 9:60: "Jesus said to let the dead bury the dead." And told us what He meant was that she could not go to Steve right then. She had to take care of the living, which meant me and the rest of the family.

She explained, "You cannot be any good to the living if you die with the dead; you are still in this life with the living." She told me that to live for the living is what we must do, and we must remember to make life count. She knew and always lived with this as her motto: "Life is too short; enjoy the ride." I heard her say that more than once, and now I know she was right.

Going through grief I learned that when things happen, reactions occur that can keep a cycle going in our lives. Then when we have triggers or limiting beliefs in our life, we will open ourselves up to be run by those things. Instead, we must see things from a different angle. The quote by William Mater Lewis can describe our life: "The tragedy of life is not that it ends too soon, but that we waited so long to begin it."

Starting today, we can begin to chart a different course and to begin a new life. We can enjoy each day, filling our lives with peace and joy and letting those spread into all other relationships. It starts with each of us. How we treat ourselves will be a factor in the way others will treat us. This is true of our children and our relationships. We must love ourselves enough to get help if needed, to get over grief, and to live for the living. I also want to add that we must give ourselves grace if it takes longer than normal to get through the process. It is *our journey*, and if it takes longer, it is imperative to give ourselves grace to get through it. Take the path and time needed to heal and recoup.

Gratitude in grief can help the process. When my mother passed away, I was 36 years old. She gave birth to me when she was 39. My immediate response to anyone who was feeling sorry for me was that I had her for 36 years – blessed years, indeed – I was thankful after losing my dad at 16 to have had the years I had with her. One never knows when a loved one will pass.

The same was true in 2021, when two of my sisters passed away back-to-back. I found something I could be grateful for, which lessened the pain. Things such as recognizing that I know people who have no siblings helped me realize, I was blessed. I got to make memories with them. I was able to sing with Jan for 50 years. That one really helped; fifty years is a long time.

We must find something other than focusing on the loss to help when we encounter grief. It will make a difference. I was thankful for the two beautiful children I got from my first marriage, for the things I learned, for the things I can see in others who are as young as I was and do not know how to continue life, for the marriage, for the divorce journey, for the hurt, for the pain, for all the things that helped make me be the person I am today. If we learn along the journey, a failure is really a learning lesson – one that hurts to the core. But one day we will be able to see all the good that came from it, even during times of grief.

LESSONS AT A GLANCE

✳ Grief comes in many forms and is a troublesome process to work through. You must go through it to *get* through it.

✳ Trust that the things needed for the journey will show up.

✳ Live for the living and give yourself grace, even when it takes time.

✳ Have gratitude through it all.

YOUR NEXT STEPS

1. Notice if you are in grief. If you are, identifying it is the first step. It is not easy, but it is a process you must go through to get through it. Seek counsel from someone who has training in grief.

2. Remember to continue to live. We must live for our loved ones. It is a choice. It is sometimes hard to see past our pain, but the living ones around us want and need us to be present.

3. Give yourself grace to find your way through. Give others (especially your children) grace through their grieving process, as well. It is everyone's own journey.

4. Have gratitude through the grief for what you learned and for what you had. Concentrate on the good that came from life and the situations. The good will help you push through.

CHAPTER 22

FINDING A TRIBE

The Alcohol Anonymous meetings have had long-time success with people fellowshipping together for a cause to overcome their drinking addiction. Teen Challenge has had success in people fellowshipping together to overcome addictions.

Through the divorce, I attended a co-dependent tribe of others who were finding themselves, who were hurting, going through divorce or a breakup. All were trying to heal. I would leave the meetings mad, upset, and feeling worse than when I went in, because the program made me deal with things I had buried.

I highly recommend finding tribes of others going through situations similar to yours. Your story may be what helps them. We all long for connections to feel we belong. We must grow in our spirit, soul, and body to maintain a life of enjoyment and to thrive. We long to be accepted as we are. We need others, whether we admit it or not.

I am currently part of a tribe called Unstoppable Influence, started by Rich and Natasha Hazlett. They have helped numerous people find their purpose and walk in it. They have also coached me and been my mentors and guides, while always displaying true love. They have inspired me to become the person God meant for me to be. When my light was very dim, my Creator put me on a path to stumble into them, and they added intense fuel to my light. I will shine brighter and keep shining bright to inspire, to encourage, and to help others along their journey in life; to be an impact maker; to be fearless; to serve; to be bold; to be imperfectly perfect; and to be a vessel of God to others.

During the most recent loss of two of my sisters, who passed away 17 days apart, this tribe played a huge part in my coming out of grief. I had a tribe praying for and supporting me. They let me talk and ugly cry, and they gave me support in a non-judgmental environment that was priceless. It helped me come out of grief faster than it otherwise would have taken. I can truly say a tribe that you can relate to and feel connected to is so valuable in both the wins and in the losses of life.

When I went through the divorce, I was in a couple of tribes. Remember the story of the bowling league I was part of? I didn't realize it then, but I was taking that time to heal and recuperate from the divorce. It was a form of self-care that I very much needed. These ladies poured love into me. A few of them had experienced divorce and their own losses and pain in similar situations. They understood where I was. I had others I could relate to who took me in and supported me. Those ladies let me vent and cry if I needed to. They supported me through an extremely hard time.

I was in a group with the therapist I saw, not only for one-on-one therapy, but for group therapy, as well. Listening and relating to the group gave us clarity on each other's pain. That is where I learned that pain comes in all sorts of packages, not just one.

We all will have gut punches in life and when we do, it helps to have those who will support and love us through it. Whether it is a church group, a group coming together to get over grief, an inspirational or uplifting group, a group of those who have lost a child – whatever you can relate to, whatever it is you need, find a group to join. It helps.

Also find a mentor. "Hear counsel, and receive instruction, that thou mayest be wise in thy latter end" (Prov. 19:20). Everyone needs a role model to remind them that if someone else can do what they need to do, they can manage it, as well. We all want to know the answers to these questions: "Can I do this? Is it possible?"

If you cannot find a tribe, start one yourself. That is what my niece Kim and I did when we were flight attendants. Jonathan and Jared were in high school, and Zach was in elementary school. We flew three weekends out of the month, and we missed being part of a tribe – that group of like-minded people who feed our souls. We could only go to church one Sunday a month, due to our schedules. So thankful for Joe he carried on as if I was there and kept the family going.

Kim and I would coordinate our schedules to be off the same weekend. We flew Thursday through Sunday, and our being away from the family caused a void not just in us, but also in our children. So, this was dual fold for our children and us. These times together held us all connected. As well as the family vacations we were able to do due to flight perks we were given.

Once a month for more than 24 months, we would come together at my house and celebrate everyone's birthdays for that month. We would do a theme each month – Mexican food, Italian food, American food, Soul food, Greek food – and we would make a huge cake to reflect the theme with everyone's names on it. We would play music that coordinated with the theme. We always had a blast.

We would have anywhere from 30 to 60 people at our house. Each month varied in crowd size, depending on what else was happening. Oh, what priceless memories we made. Our doors were open to everyone, my ex-husband came to several dinners to celebrate the boys' birthdays, Joe's ex-wife came to many dinners for the twins and for Zach. My sister's ex-husband and his family would come when it was their children's birthday. We even celebrated the ex's birthdays.

We had people tell us, "Y'all are weird!" They did not understand how we could intermingle with our ex-family members. But it was not about us, it was about the children. This idea came because we felt left out, like we were missing out on connections. We needed to get our fix to be able to go the rest of the month. It kept us motivated; it kept us excited, and it kept the connections going that we so longed for.

Another perk of having a large family is that everyone would bring a dish to go with the theme, and we always had food left over. We had laughter, intimate connections with others, and a sense of belonging. We were able to love others. Knowing we were loved was what we needed to thrive. We were also contributing to a bigger cause than ourselves. We were certain everyone else needed what we needed, and we all benefited from it.

I share this story to show it is possible to build a tribe for whatever it is you need. A lot of times we will not move if we cannot find what we need. Let's create what we need, instead. It is possible to make it happen.

As each one of our family members passed away, I became so grateful for those memories we made over the years together. We had enough devastating moments to last a lifetime, so we created those priceless moments that would also last a lifetime. It was also a learning experience for our family that "crap happens," but you can be civil and go on with your life.

LESSONS AT A GLANCE

❋ Finding your tribe can be an effective way to gain the support, love, and understanding you need through life circumstances, trials, and pain to heal from emotional wounds.

❋ If you cannot find a tribe, start one.

❋ Recognize that children need tribes and support as well.

YOUR NEXT STEPS

1. Finding the right tribe for you may take a few meetings with a few tribes, but they are out there. Successes have come from AA and Teen Challenge, and I can tell you personally the tribe I was in last year during grief was the best thing at the time to pull me out faster. Find a tribe to connect with where you are and see how it can help.

2. If there is not a tribe in your city for you, create one. We are not the only ones that hurt. Everyone hurts from time to time. Others need us, and we need others. Remember that every tribe starts with someone taking the initiative. You can be that someone.

CHAPTER 23

DECLARE AND DECREE

"Thou shall also decree a thing, and it shall be established unto thee: and the light shall shine upon thy ways" (Job 22:28). Declare and decree, and it shall come to pass. This was a step I learned to put in place while believing for my children and accepting the principle behind it. It is the same as asking, believing, and receiving.

We must declare how we will be as a person, a family unit, a business, or anything we want or attempt to do. Decreeing means establishing it. When we declare, decree, and have determination, I believe we can manage anything that comes our way. We are working in faith, and we know the outcome. "For out of the abundance of the heart the mouth speaketh" (Matt. 12:34).

We have settled it. We say what we want, we act as if it is ours. When I believed for my children, I had to act as if it was done. I bought baby clothes, and I knew in my heart I would have children. That is how they were manifested to me. I declared, I decreed, and it was settled.

How quickly we can forget this concept. After I went through the divorce, it seemed I quit decreeing. I settled in the belief that life was happening *to* me, not *for* me. That is when I started counseling. I knew life was not meant to be lived miserably. I had precious gifts – my children – whom I knew were answered prayers.

I decreed a good help mate and Joe showed up. I pushed him away for over a year. I could not see us in a relationship together. We did get together, and it started out wonderfully. However, when I encountered the pain of a stepchild not liking me, I again quickly forgot how to decree. I was ready to run.

Thankfully, Joe took the lead. Joe always said, "The main thing is, do not panic." When anything comes our way, staying grounded in our hope in God is key. The event is either to teach us a lesson, to strengthen our faith or to test us. Again, we are stronger than we think we are. "I can do all things through Christ who strengthens me" (Phil. 4:13). Joe reminded me that if we kept our lens, our perspective, our views free and clear and refused to let them get cloudy with fear, doubt, or bitterness – all the things that could cloud them – then we could get through anything.

He said, "Our focus is one day getting to the front porch with healthy, vibrant children and grandchildren and then looking back over our lives, knowing we lived them as we wanted to, we loved each other through it all, and we survived what a lot of couples would not because we would not throw in the towel and give up." He was persistent in his faith in God, in us, and in our children. Thankfully, he would not let me quit. Joe always kept our focus on the bigger picture.

No lesson or experience is wasted if we learn, we grow, and we share from those experiences. All past experiences, good and bad, have lessons that emerged from them. Those lessons have sharpened you to make you who you are today. It is important to recognize that no matter who we are today or where we are in the journey of life, we must make it a point to work on ourselves in order to be the greatest person we can be, to be our best in our relationships, and, at the same time, to be authentic to ourselves.

Thriving in life requires us to embrace our values and to continue learning, growing, and understanding how we can be our best selves. This, in turn, is reflected in the children in our lives and in our family legacy. A dedication to being a great role model, with the acceptance of our own imperfections and commitment to ourselves, will open doors and understanding.

Along this journey, we must never lose our hope. Hold onto hope, for hope is the thing, when ignited by faith, that can and will bring all things into our lives. "Faith is the substance of things hoped for, the evidence of things not seen" (Heb. 11:1).

Abraham's Faith

Abraham in the Bible is an example to follow. Notice how God painted the picture for Abraham. Abraham believed it and it came to pass.

In Genesis Chapter 17 the Bible says, "And I will make a covenant between me and thee and will multiply thee. Thou shalt be a father of many nations."

Abraham believed God. He stayed strong in his faith, and Romans 4 tells us that because he did not stagger in his faith but believed, what he believed for came about. "(As it is written, I have made thee a father of many nations,) before Him Whom he believed, *even* God, who quickeneth the dead, and called those things which be not as though they were" (Rom. 4:17).

We must walk out our proclamation, just like Abraham did. Hope and faith are still the same today and will bring about the completion of everything we are believing for.

Paint the picture you need to be secure in your faith. By faith, when God called Abraham out to go to a place he would receive as his inheritance, Abraham obeyed and went, even though he did not know where he was going. Abraham taught us how to walk: in faith.

ABRAHAM STEPS:

- God told Abraham he would be a father of many nations. If it is in God's Word, we, too, can have what He says. Search out the Word for what you are wanting.
- Abraham did not stagger in his belief but knew the thing God told him would come about. We, too, can lock in and know that things will come about in our lives.
- Abraham called those things that were not as though they were. Confessions, affirmations, and actions work by calling those things that are not in existence into our possession. Faith without action is dead. (I bought baby clothes before I was a mother, I believed God.)
- What Abraham believed came about. What I believed came about. What you believe for can also come about. Faith works!

CHAPTER 24

YOUR FOCUS AND YOUR FAITH

I have heard it said over and over in my life that no man can define who we are. It is up to us. One of my favorite quotes ever is, "If it's to be, it's up to me," by William Johnsen. *What defines you?*

Limiting beliefs are things that can define us and limit us. Limiting beliefs are anything we believe to be true that is not in actuality absolute truth. For example, I could have locked into my doctor's belief and never had children. We are limited when we do not dig deep and find out who we are, what our purpose is, what our visions are, what our dreams and aspirations are. We must stay true to those against all odds. Stay the course and watch what can happen in your life.

This is so true. Go after the life of happiness you want, pursue your heart's desires, stay true to your Creator, and watch how life can, and will open for you. We often get stuck in ourselves and worry about what other people think. In life, I have also found it to be true that most people do not even care what is going on with us. They have their own stuff with which they are dealing. A lot of times, even the ones we are closest to are not paying any attention. They are focused on their own lives, as well.

If we are lucky, we will have those who love us no matter what, and they will stand with us through whatever we go through in life. They will coach us, be our friends, and love us throughout our entire lives. God, however, will conspire to help us and take us through whatever we are going through. Through prayer, the Word of God, and faith, seek the truth. Once truth comes, action upon the truth is key. Faith without DOING the work is dead; nothing will happen.

It is the same in everything we want to do. We can think about losing weight and eating healthily, but unless we implement the necessary steps, we will never lose a pound. We must acquire mastery of our own live and continue to feed your faith. Faith comes by repetitively hearing the Word of God, learning about other people's successes, and asking for the right books to be placed in our path. They will come.

Then move. Take the action steps required to do whatever it is you want to do. I like to say, *"Get pregnant with the thing,"* whether it is a successful family, a goal, a dream, a vision, or whatever it is. When you conceive it, and you nurture it until it is birthed, it is yours. All the steps to getting that baby will be worth all the things it took to get it.

I encourage you to dig out the individual answers you need in your own life's journey. It is time to be courageous and fearless. If you do not believe you can be successful, you will never succeed. Devour the books, paint the picture, and give yourself permission. It will happen. Never waver. Teach your children this concept, knowing that they are watching you. That is one of the most valuable lessons you can teach them.

As you have read in this book, you can overcome all obstacles that you will meet in life, whether it is getting over devastation in your life such as divorce or the loss of a loved one; moving through the creation of a blended family; or making sure your personal life or your dreams get off the ground. I had a vision for this book, and I had to look to mentors to get the confidence I needed to complete it. It took challenging work and digging to find the right mentors and the right answers. The struggle is real, but it is worth it. Once the thing we believed for becomes tangible and rests in our hands, all the anguish is diminished.

Thus, focus and faith will make us wealthy in all aspects of our lives. The definition of wealth is not limited to monetary terms. There is also wealth in love, wealth in relationships, and wealth in peace that comes by trusting your God. This is true success to me. The richest people in the world, like Mother Teresa and Billy Graham, were rich in love and in serving others.

The ability to do this also depends on deciding to be the victor and to face our fears. We have a choice in life of whether to stay a victim or be a victor. What do you choose? Sometimes we express our need for love and belonging in the opposite way of what we really want. We act out in ways of self-destruction or self-sabotage. When fear talks, it can be dangerous. Anytime fear leads us to decide something, generally, it is not a good decision.

Self-fulfilling prophecies happen. For instance, saying, "I knew this would not work," or "I knew this was too good to be true," can start a decline in a relationship that will ultimately end the relationship. But keeping your focus on things such as "For God hath not given us the spirit of fear; but of power, and of love and of a sound mind" (2 Tim. 1:7) these things can help us remember to be the victor; to stay present and to remember to breathe.

We must give ourselves the gift of living in the present and letting life produce for us the results we need. Staying present in your life and realizing what we think about grows. If we focus on avoiding pain, then more pain shows up. Think positive thoughts instead. A worthwhile life is worth putting effort and time into, so focus on capturing memories, creating friendships for life (that includes your spouse and your children) and finding tribes that support you in changing the world, one person at a time.

When we think of our journey and only look at the hard parts of our lives, the hard will become our focus. It can become a drudgery and a challenge that looks impossible to get through. If we look at our journey as it will be supplied for by our Creator, we do not need to know how or what is possible, we only need to know it is possible, trusting that our Creator has us and will lead us and guide us for our good. With that perspective, the journey becomes easier. The gifts begin to show up and the how, the what, and the possible happen.

LESSONS AT A GLANCE

✱ Go after the life of happiness you want, pursue your heart's desires, stay true to your Creator, and watch how life can and will open up for you.

✱ Your focus and your faith define you and can make you wealthy in all areas of your life.

✱ You can choose your role as the victim or the victor.

✱ What we think about and focus on becomes prominent in our lives, so focus on positive thoughts.

YOUR NEXT STEPS

1. Take a genuine look at your life to determine where your focus is and where your faith level is. Who are you, really? What are you focused on? What do you believe? Where is your faith level in the things you are believing for? Take an evaluation and see where you truly are.

2. What actions are you doing, or can you do, to move your goals, your dreams, and your family in the direction you want to go? Small steps daily will get you there.

3. "Get pregnant" with the thing. (Whatever the "thing" is.)

4. Paint the picture and give yourself permission to have what it is you are believing for. Then, never quit and never waver in it.

CHAPTER 25

A NEW YOU

I remember wanting to reset and having my plan backfire, yet it became a lesson on "what not to do." I had the idea that if I changed my appearance, it would help me be the person I wanted to be. Looking back, I realize this was funny. Basic truth: we will still be the same person, no matter how we change our looks. Without a behavior change, we are still the same.

A new you — a reset — is up to you! We can always reset our lives. If we are not going in the direction we want to go in, it is up to us to decide to change direction.

When I turned 40, I wanted something new, a "new me" look, and I wanted to *feel* new again. It was time for a remake of myself. I knew life offered more than what I was experiencing. Again, a longing in me was showing up. I saw Susan Powter, an Australian-born motivational speaker who used the phrase "Stop the Insanity" in her weight loss informercial. I loved her haircut and thought it was what I wanted. I went to the beauty shop, got my hair cut one inch all over my head and colored it blonde. I thought it would look cute and create a new me.

Wrong! The haircut looked cute on her, but *awful* on me. Joe looked at me when I got home and said, "You have ruined yourself." I had wanted to change some insanity, but instead I created more. It was horrible.

We were having a baby shower at our church for a young lady and when I walked in, I put on an act as though I loved my new appearance. No one will ever think anything about my looks, my life, or what I have on, I thought, if I act as though this is what I wanted. So that's what I did. I was not going to let anyone know that I was aware how horrible it was. I sat beside the grandmother of our church, Lois Stover, who was around 70 at this time. She had beady-looking eyes when she was serious about something, and with those eyes, she said, "You know you do not like that mess!" I said, "You are so right, but no one else here is going to know it." The way we perceive ourselves is how others perceive us. If people thought I liked my new look, they liked it, too. If I let them know that I hated it, they would have hated it, as well.

Be careful of the authority you give to others. I knew my hair would grow back, and it did. Another lesson in the books for me. Looks cannot define who we are or change us. Man cannot define us. Situations and circumstances cannot define us. If I had just waited it out a few years, I would have wound up wearing that hair style out of necessity after I experienced a brain bleed and had to have surgery. The second time, my hair was gray instead of blonde. It was still horrible. Yet, it still did not define me.

One of my nephews, as he was being potty trained, had an "experience" one day. My sister walked out of the bathroom for just a moment, and when she returned, he had poop everywhere. It was all over the potty chair, in his hair, on the floor, on the walls. My sister learned a lesson rather quickly, and she never left his younger brothers alone when they were on the pot. Our lives can be like that but, happily, we can get rid of the nasty things that do not serve us and get free. If we think negatively, those thoughts can quickly rub off on everything, just like that poop. This is why we must reset our limiting thoughts, as well as our beliefs.

Our thoughts matter. What are your thoughts on your family? What are your thoughts on your children or stepchildren? What are your thoughts on your spouse, your situation, your life? The Bible tells us what to think in Philippians 4:8 "Finally, brethren, whatever things are true, whatever things are honest, whatever things are just, whatever things are pure, whatever things are lovely, whatever things are of good report; if there is any virtue, and if there be any praise, think on these things."

Poop thoughts produce poop everywhere. What is said in our head matters. Then we must watch what we say aloud. "Thou art snared with the words of thy mouth, thou art taken with the words of thy mouth" (Prov. 6:2). So, once we figure out what it is we want, and we find the backing of the Word, we must watch what we say from that point on. Our words can nullify our faith and set us back. If we say, "I will never get it," then we will never get it.

I remember when I disliked my stepson and was so distraught that I had chosen this journey to be with his dad. I was miserable and unhappy. I had no peace, no joy. Sure, I loved him, but loving and liking someone are different. I did not like the anguish I felt and was going through. At that time, I could not look past the problem to see that gifts were present. I could only see the situation (the poop), and I wanted to run away.

I had been a hider for several years until I saw a therapist who called me out from behind the door. I wanted to go back into hiding. [3] That story is in the book "Free to Be Me," a compilation of stories written by Unstoppable Influencers. I highly recommend the book. It has stories shared by numerous women who were set free from their limiting beliefs. As I said at the beginning of the book, you can be set free as well.

My husband had lovingly said we needed to make our marriage work. We muddled through our limiting beliefs and hurdles one at a time and, trust me, we had many over our 31-year journey. However, our joys far exceed any of the challenges and hurts we faced through the journey. I know that once you decide, if you stick to it, trust God, and ask Him for guidance and wisdom, the process will hand you gifts. I thank God for the gifts of my journey, and you will be able to say the same thing.

All my life I have heard that things happen for a reason. I believe that to be true. Either we are growing, learning, and sharing, or we are repeating a process. If we do not learn the lessons we need to learn, we will keep going through the same old same old until we do. I also learned we have no rights over another person's choices. If they do not willfully agree with you, it is OK. They have that right. We have no right to force our beliefs, our passions, or our visions on anyone. We can always agree to disagree.

Everyone has heard what insanity is. As Einstein said, it is "doing the same thing over and over again and expecting different results." If we keep doing the same old things, we must ask ourselves why we are doing this. Ask not in a negative frame of mind, such as "poor me," but in a positive state. The right questions get the right answers. "What is it I need to learn? What are the lessons here?" Ask, believe, and receive that the answers are open to you, and they will be. Take the attitude of a student, never be too big to ask questions, and never know too much to be open to learning something new.

We must believe that and know our journey is getting better every day. We must keep standing until the completion of the thing we are believing for. It will happen. I have a life of passion and love, and my cup runs over. So can yours.

LESSONS AT A GLANCE

❋ We can always reset our lives.

❋ Our thoughts and words matter.

❋ The right questions get the right answers.

❋ Once we make a decision, if we stick to it, trust God, and ask Him for guidance and wisdom, the process will hand us gifts.

YOUR NEXT STEPS

1. Think about what needs to be reset in your life. Take an evaluation and identify the things that need to be reset. Remember that this is not a one-time thing. We must continually evaluate and adjust.

2. Figure out who you really are. What are you here for? What do you want? What do you desire? No one can figure that out but you.

3. Get laser-focused on keeping your thoughts in check. Think good thoughts and praise your way to the completion of the things you are believing for.

4. Watch what you say. You can nullify everything you're believing for with your mouth. Only say what coincides with the result you want.

5. Make a decision, stick to it, trust God, and ask Him for guidance and wisdom.

CHAPTER 26

TAKING CARE OF RELATIONSHIPS

When you succeed in your relationships at home, relationships outside the home become easier. You do not become happy by being negative about your children or your marriage. When you have a strong family life, you receive the message that you are loved, you are cared for, and you are important. It is important to take care of all your relationships and learn to protect them.

There are two prominent fears that can start early in childhood, especially in children of divorced parents or with those who are adopted. These are the fear of not being enough and the fear of not being loved. This all starts in the home. A blended family has its own baggage from all parties who have been brought to the home; however, love, kindness, trust, and sometimes counseling, as I have mentioned, can and will prevail.

To have a solid family and a healthy marriage, we must work hard at creating them. Feeling appreciated and accepted and being treated kindly as part of a loving family are things so very vital to all humans. We must have a supportive environment to learn to thrive, rather than merely to survive. Our past can poison our future if we stay mired in the past. Love can change the atmosphere and cause others to be the best version of themselves. I have seen that in action, as well. A love relationship does not just happen; it can be created by a soft-spoken answer. "A soft answer turneth away wrath: but grievous words stir up anger" (Prov. 15:1).

Love changed the atmosphere in our home. In my previous example, Chris hated me, literally. However, love prevailed and ultimately won. One hundred years from now, will any of these things matter? Absolutely. A family's legacy can be changed. Our families are worth fighting for. Our children are worth being an example for. Our country needs us to step up and be *strong* families – the kind that learn to fight for what is right at home. If we win the world but lose our children, have we truly won?

Our spouses are worth fighting for. We must make time for our spouse. The outside environment seeks out those who are lonely, those who are not satisfied. Satisfy your spouse by taking the time to make love and enjoy each other. Keep your husband or wife satisfied. They belong to you and want to feel loved, sexy, and appreciated. It makes a difference. Whisper sexy innuendos to your spouse from time to time. Keep the romance alive, and your spouse will not have a reason to seek it out elsewhere. One of the reasons Joe and I have been successful is that he has always been available for me, and I have been available for him.

Remember that happiness is a choice. We can be happy when we transform our view of any relationship. External is never the answer. Internally is where you start. The difference between joy and happiness is an internal feeling that we choose to walk in, regardless of our circumstances and what we have or do not have. Feelings of being annoyed, anxious, or empty of joy are internal. It is up to us to find our joy and keep it. Happiness can be affected by outside forces. I am not happy if I get a speeding ticket. I am happy when my husband brings me flowers, or my child gets As on his report card.

Neither the world system, the government, or what we do for a living is our source; God is.

What we do for a living is a vehicle given to us that will provide the means to live, but it is ultimately not our Source. When we choose to have our number one relationship with God intact, everything flows better in our lives. Relationships have a way of working themselves out when God is foremost and center in our lives. Money cannot buy the power of God. It is manifested to us through faith. That faith manifested in us is where peace of mind, a clear conscience, mental stability, and love come from. These things are given to us to be released to others. When love flows through us, we will see our lives and other lives transformed.

When we choose to walk in joy and to keep joy at all costs – knowing our Creator is in us and working all things for our good – we can keep our peace. Joy can make us smile when someone says something ugly to us, because we know they are not living in joy. Maybe such a circumstance is a suitable time to share a story with them about joy and how to acquire it and keep it.

Deep down, joy and knowing who we are can help us treat others with kindness, even when they really do not deserve it. When we understand joy, and the difference in joy and happiness, we can see it has an influence in all our relationships. If we want to have true influence in our families, with our friends, and across our sphere of influence, we must walk in joy.

Protecting All Your Relationships

One of my coaches had a good metaphor. She said, "Imagine you are on one end of a line and on the other end of the line is your significant other, your children, your friends, your family, your coworkers, and the space in the middle of the line is symbolic of the relationships. When the space in the middle is protected and you are mindful of keeping that space unbroken and thriving, you can keep relationships."

She also said, "Imagine your relationships as a houseplant. When you water, feed, and protect it, that plant can live for years. If you do not protect it, you accidentally put poison on it, do not water it, or do not give it sunshine, it will die." That is true in all our relationships. If we start accusing and wounding the other parties, if we are jealous, if we keep strife going, then we will kill our relationships. Abuse of any kind will diminish our relationship. Communication must be kept open. When we feed the relationship with good, good will come out of it.

I like to think of every person and every relationship as a field. We are surrounded by corn fields, soybeans, and cotton fields where I live. The farmer treats the soil with hydrogen, fertilizers, and lime to prepare it for a great harvest. Then when the seeds are planted, along with the addition of sunshine and of rain and the effort of keeping the weeds out, that field will produce a bountiful harvest. We also must tend to our personal fields to be able to give good out to others and produce a harvest. Prayer, meditation, exercise, and reading good books are what help reproduce a bountiful harvest in our lives.

Likewise, it is up to us to feed our children and show them how to tend their personal fields as they grow to be able to give to others. Our energy field is real, and it should be nurtured and tended to; otherwise, we will live in lack, which is not what our Creator wants for us.

A lot of times when a blended family comes together, the merging fields are depleted without manifesting any clue what is wrong with them. Work is essential in the blend to till and fertilize the soil until it starts producing a harvest. Keep in mind that the harvest sometimes takes years. I have witnessed, firsthand, fields that were tended to and still never produced a harvest. I am sure you have, too. However, I feel we should do our best to help every field produce a bountiful crop. If some fields never produce, then we must simply let them go.

My mother, when she was about to pass on from Lou Gehrig's Disease, would not let go until I promised her that I would look after my middle brother. She had tended his field, as he could not mentally or emotionally do so himself. She wanted to make sure someone had him before she let go. A powerful lesson was passed on to me during that time.

I remember another time when I was 17 and was in a wreck. I stopped about a foot from hitting a tree, which would have injured me very badly. One of my brothers-in-law accused me of driving too fast around the curve; however, the truth was, I had gone to sleep at the wheel. His accusations offended me for a long time because he would not hear me or let me speak. His response was always, "No, I know you were driving too fast."

That assumption, though incorrect, cut deep into me. It was like cutting ruts in my field. I eventually had a confrontation with him about it because it ate at me; it shut me down.

Tearing people down can shut a person off completely, hindering their spiritual walk and all their other relationships. When we change our actions and the way we treat others, love will begin to shine through. Being authentic and real in relationships strengthens those relationships.

Relationships need to be strong because children need both parents if issues are to be worked out. It is mostly trivial stuff that causes rifts. It can also be a deep, underlying problem, such as individual core issues or spiritual issues. I suggest, at all costs, if parents can work out their differences, they should work them out. That is so unless drugs, abuse of any kind – physical, mental, or sexual – are involved. In those circumstances, please get professional help to get the child in a safe place to grow up and to know what is and is not acceptable. Our children should be kept in a safe environment.

I had a friend once whom I really cared for and loved. However, she had been sexually abused by her stepdad for years. She would only let people get so close to her. As soon as she felt someone was invading her space, she would snap at them. It was like rubbing a dog and expecting it to like the attention, but finding that, instead, the animal would turn on you, growl, and run off. My friend and I tried to laugh often together because the other choice was to cry. She refused to talk about the negative things in her life. She would not allow me to get close to her. She never got to the root cause of her not loving herself or letting anyone really love her. Sadly, she passed away without ever dealing with her pain.

If you know someone like this, try to encourage them to see a therapist; maybe their wounds can be healed. Mark Twain once said, "Anger is an acid that can do more harm to the vessel in which it is stored than to anything on which it is poured." Hate and bitterness are not worth carrying around. We must let go of them. It is so important to latch onto the positive, versus locking in on the negative and getting negative results. In this life, the negative is everywhere. It is up to us to find the positive and to tune out the negative.

I want to encourage you to focus on your words, your thoughts, and your actions. Take control of your life. This, in turn, is going to strengthen the family dynamic. Our children learn so much from what they see us do – how we act and react. They are watching, even when we do not realize it. They are sponges that soak up their surroundings. Be positive and let them witness that mindset and soak it up.

In addition, we need to keep our emotions in check. I remember being emotionally starved, and I went looking for my emotions to be fed. I finally learned to seek first to fill the perceived gap with my Creator before looking to someone or something else. God can fill our cups, and He can lead us on the path of fulfillment in every area of our lives.

Life does not have to be a struggle. It is up to us, and it does not matter where we are now or where we have been. We can create the life we want by making different choices. All our relationships should be full of passion.

We get anxious in life with our spouses, our children, and our other relationships, but we must realize life is short. Sometimes it takes life-shaking experiences to wake us up. Let us not wait for those moments, but let's decide today to live a life by design — a life beyond our wildest dreams. Focus, set with intention and faith, is key. "With men this is impossible; but with God all things are possible" (Matt. 19:26).

We cannot ever judge another person; it is never truly possible to understand the pain and obstacles they have navigated on their unique path of life. Keep in mind that where we come from does not determine where we are going.

I will say as far as you and your spouse, always remain true best friends with each other. I can honestly say Joe and I are best friends. Our relationship was tried many times, but because we were friends, we broke through barriers that might not otherwise have been broken through. Our friendship prevailed. We have had lots of laughter together over the years. When it seems like life is getting extra hard, we always manage to break away and remember to laugh. Laughter really is like medicine "A merry heart doeth good like a medicine: But a broken spirit drieth the bones" (Prov. 17:22).

Remember to have date nights with your spouse to nurture your relationship and stay connected. When the children are grown it will be just you two together again. I have known marriages that have split up after the children were grown because the couple no longer knew who the other person was, and they were too far apart to come back together.

I will never forget how I felt when I heard those words: "*I hate you!*" Hate is so harsh, and I did not know what to do with those words or the child from whom the words were coming. I know that without Joe saying "No" to my walking away, I would have walked. Be the person in your family to take a stand. Change can come for you and your family. Small steps can lead to huge successes. Creating a mental picture of your family getting better every day is a terrific way to start. Reading other stories of successful families is a wonderful way to stay motivated. Inspiration can come in many forms. Find what works for you to stay on course.

I love it when our children call just to chat or stop in on Saturday morning for a cup of coffee. Nothing is more fulfilling. Parenting is not easy. Adulting is not, either. Be Real. Be you. Love your children and extend grace when needed. As a reminder, we are not perfect human beings. We were once children with imperfections, and we are not perfect as grown-ups, either. But God loves us through our imperfections. Let's love our children through theirs.

LESSONS AT A GLANCE

❋ When we succeed in our relationships at home, relationships outside the home become easier.

❋ Our families, children, and spouses are worth fighting for.

❋ Happiness is a choice.

❋ Protect all your relationships.

❋ All our relationships should be full of passion.

❋ Change can come for you and your family. Be the person in your family to take a stand.

❋ Be who you are and say what you feel. Be real. Be you. Be a true servant of God! Let your children be themselves, as well.

YOUR NEXT STEPS

1. Figure out how to operate in love in the home, treating everyone with respect, acceptance, appreciation. What does your family need to get there? Have family meetings, if something gets off balance, to keep everyone in check.

2. Happiness is a choice. Decide to be happy. Get deep joy embedded in your spirit.

3. Protect all your relationships at all costs. What can you do to pay attention to the individuals around you and see if their fields are depleted?

4. Instead of demanding change, be real about what the issue is and about what may occur if the problem is not stopped or fixed. This approach can easily resolve issues and stop problems. Get real and raw with all parties and let them know your feelings. Hear their feelings, as well. A reminder truth is what brings the lasting change to our lives.

5. Change can and will come to your home when the passion for life is present in you. Others respond to passion and love. Be the person in your family to take a stand.

6. Give yourself permission to be who you are and say what you feel. Be real. Be you. Be a true servant of God!

CHAPTER 27

DEAR STEPPARENT

A letter written by a stepparent. Notice what she wished she had known prior to stepping into the stepparent role. I almost feel as if I am writing in a diary, telling my newly engaged self what I needed to hear. I wish I had received a letter like this during that time. It would have made such a difference.

Dear Stepparent,

You are always one to put yourself in everyone's shoes, so that you are sure to do the right thing. Truth is, when it comes to this many people, all with different feelings, it is impossible to make everyone happy. Everyone will have their turn getting their feelings hurt, but it is not about you. It is about the child. Being a stepparent is hard, but your job as a stepparent, aside from putting God first, is to put your marriage and the children, including the stepchildren, before anyone else. ANYONE. Do what is best for the child no matter how hard the situation is. Respect healthy boundaries but do not make yourself uncomfortable to make someone else comfortable. Someone else's opinion of you is none of your business. Talk it over with God first. Sometimes being the bigger person means not putting yourself in situations you know will cause drama, and in a blended family, a lot of things that should not cause drama, do. You only have the power to change your heart and actions. I know you will refuse to let your heart grow cold over someone else's actions. This blended family is a blessing in disguise. You are receiving from God someone you never thought you needed. Be the role model, the best version of yourself to the children, all parents involved, and be the friend you always needed. Enjoy that sweet blessing and all their future milestones!

Love, Montana[4]

YOUR NEXT STEPS

What would your letter look like; a letter to yourself as a stepparent? What are the things you would say? Write them down. prayerfully ponder over the words, the actions, the things you wish you had known, the joys you have experienced, the grief that you have experienced from blending the family together. Then release yourself to be the best stepmom ever.

CHAPTER 28

LIVING A LIFE OF HARMONY

"The thief cometh not, but for to steal, and to kill, and to destroy: I am come that they might have life, and that they might have it more abundantly" (John 10:10).

That we stay in a state of harmony is God's perfect will for us. That does not mean having all we want. Rather, it is living in a state of enjoyment for all we have been given. Things change. Seasons change. However, the state of fully enjoying life is one we all strive to reach.

We can get so caught up in living our day-to-day activities that sometimes we are functioning, but not really *living*. I have coached couples who are so caught up in the moments of life, they only see their circumstances. They lose precious time with family because of this. They forget each other. They forget that children need them. They forget self-care and the fact that they need to tend to themselves to be able to give to others. "Thou shalt love thy neighbor as thyself" (Matt. 22:39).

Love starts with each of us. Which means we must love ourselves. Nurture your spirit, soul, and body to be able to give to others. I want to encourage you to set aside time to feed yourself spiritually, as well as physically, to be able to tackle life.

Your soul, your mind, your will, and your emotions need good stuff to grow and to help you stay attentive and in the present. Make the most of where you are today.

Love the ones who are in your life and create rapport with even the smallest member of the family. Then you will have lasting relationships without regrets. I know people who feel they wasted years on a relationship when it ends, especially if it was a toxic relationship. My mother, for example, spent years with my dad after he came back from World War II. He had become an alcoholic. I asked her why she stayed with him. She replied, "I knew the real Joe before he went to war." She loved the real Joe, the man who was lost in the war. I asked her years later if she regretted it, and her reply was that she did not. She stayed true to him until he passed away. Why? Because love sees past flaws; love sees the heart. She had no regrets.

To be free, we must learn how to let go. Refuse to entertain your old pain. We waste a lot of energy hanging onto the past. The past can hold you back from becoming a new you. The past does not define you or your direction. If we know we are imperfect beings, realize that we make mistakes, and admit we do not know everything, then we must be willing to accept our shortcomings. Our lives can then be different. I have never met a perfect person.

We must have the attitude that if we are not perfect, then we must allow others to be imperfect, to an extent. (Again, abuse is never to be accepted.) If someone has hurt you, go to them, if possible. Release the hurt done against you and let it go. Offenses can dry up our happiness and our joy. The journey will not be easy, but the rewards and the gifts along the way are more than worth it.

LESSONS AT A GLANCE

✻ Staying in a state of harmony is God's perfect will for us.

✻ Love starts with each of us.

✻ To live in harmony, we must let go of past pain.

✻ Accept your imperfections and those of others, as well.

YOUR NEXT STEPS

1. The price Jesus paid for us to have life and life abundant is enough to know a state of harmony is possible for us. It is a choice on our part to get there and live there.

2. Love yourself first – which means taking care of your body, mind and soul – so you will have something to give others.

3. Allow others to make mistakes but release the hurt from those mistakes so offenses do not build. See if there are wounds or mistakes from others that you need to release. If possible, have that conversation and clear the offense. Release yourself to be the free person you are meant to be, living your best life on your terms and with no one holding you in bondage.

CHAPTER 29

SHARING THE MESSAGE

In Luke 7:22, Jesus says go and tell what things you have seen and heard. Romans 10:13-18 says, "For whosoever shall call on the name of the Lord shall be saved. How then shall they call on Him in Whom they have not believed? And how shall they believe in Him of Whom they have not heard? And how shall they hear without a preacher?"

If we do not shout out our wins, how will others know? If we do not release our words to others, are we not like the lepers who were all healed, yet only one came back to thank Jesus, as it is recorded in Luke 17:15. Let's be the ones who follow our Creator and share how He has performed in our lives. Once you overcome something, you should tell someone about your victory. Shout it from the rooftop so to speak so others can shout too.

When we want to do anything in life, one of the first things we do is look and see if anyone has already done it. If so, we can, too. We must share our stories. Knowing others have conquered divorce and became stepmothers built the belief in me that I could, too.

Sharing our journeys is the only way someone will ever hear our stories. It is *your* story, and every story is different. How can we help someone unless we share? The journeys we all go on are rough, and as I explained, pain is pain, no matter how you get it. Success and wins can come only with faith, determination, and forward movement.

When we get stuck in life without a lifeline or knowledge about how to escape the mess, hopelessness can set in. In order to help others, we must be willing to be vulnerable and share the things we once did not know, the things that embarrass us, the things that represent our weak moments as well as our mountaintop experiences.

I had two brothers who were divorced and due to the divorces, they could never pick themselves up to live again. Their lives pretty much ended when the divorces happened, and it was no one's fault but their own. They never had the faith or the fire in them to continue and to get unstuck. It broke all our hearts.

We cannot do anything for another person except to inspire and uplift them, encourage change in their lives, and create a vision that they, too, can live a life beyond their wildest dreams – a life full of love and passion.

Our lives are the sum of the people, the events, the situations, the lessons, the pain, the growing, and all the circumstances that come into our lives. The stories we hear also affect our total being. If we hear a story and can relate to it and if the story has a hero ending, it clarifies that we, too, can be the hero.

Let's spread the message of our wins to help others spread the message of their wins. We can light a fire where we are. We can be not only the hero in our own stories, but we can help others to be heroes. We can make a difference.

Sharing our wins as a family is something we started doing about a year ago. My mentor often talked about celebrating wins, and we started sharing our daily wins or challenges with the family around the supper table.

It is so funny how children pick up on the smallest things that change. Recently our 6-year-old grandson, who is at our table almost daily, said, "Maw-Maw, you did not ask me about my win today." He has already recognized that win's matter. Sharing our wins opens the door for even more wins in our lives.

LESSONS AT A GLANCE:

❖ Tell someone about your wins. Embrace and celebrate them.

❖ Sharing our journeys is the only way someone will ever hear our stories.

❖ Being the hero of our stories shows others they can be the hero of their stories.

❖ Sharing wins as a family can make for special lessons and memories.

YOUR NEXT STEPS

1. Tell someone about your wins. Embrace and celebrate them.

2. What is your story? Who can you share it with? Can you write a book? Can you share with others as you know their struggles?

3. Implanting a dream should be our moral obligation when we see someone down and out. Make a commitment, if you hear about or know someone struggling with the things you have struggled with, to share your story with them so they, too, can get free.

4. You can light a fire. Not only can you be the hero in your story, but you can help others to be a hero. One story, one person, one hero at a time can make a difference.

5. Share your wins as a family, and have it become a part of your routine.

CHAPTER 30

STAYING IN UNITY

Nothing ever comes and stays without a test to see if we are going to hold onto our wins. We must fight for our wins and maintain our ground to gain more ground. It will take determination and a decision to "Stay in UNITY," no matter what comes at us.

I like to think of UNITY as: YOU AND I TIED TOGETHER.

There is no untying what we have tied together with God. We made the decision to stand upon Him, and we will not be broken.

A person standing alone can be attacked and defeated, but two can stand back-to-back and conquer. "And if one prevail against him, two shall withstand him; and a threefold cord is not quickly broken (Eccl 4:12)."

Unity means the state of being united or joined as a whole. The state of one; oneness. A whole or totality, as combining all its parts into one. With God walking beside us, Jesus interceding for us and Holy Spirit within us we have what we need to succeed at everything we set out to do.

The family has come together as one. No matter the storms that blow, how low the valleys may be, or how high the mountains that stand before us, we have decided we are in this to win and will stick together through it all.

We are now a united family; it has become *"us"*. We are individuals in the family but, ultimately, the family is *us*. We determine our family unit and how we will be – a strong family that is harmonious and thriving.

Strong families make strong cities and, ultimately, will make a strong nation.

LESSONS AT A GLANCE

❊ A family must come together in unity and stay in unity.

❊ Make the decision to stick together. Individuals together create the "us."

YOUR NEXT STEPS

1. Pray and ask God to tie you and your family together with a cord that cannot be broken. Make the commitment to God, to yourself, to your family, and to your story. Write your life as you want it to be.

2. Have a conversation with all the family members, explaining that as a family, you and your spouse have decided – with God as the intertwining cord holding you together – that you will stick together through all that comes at you, no matter what.

CONCLUSION

In life, you will always be tried. You will always be learning, growing, or sharing. Life will hand you many things that you do not want. Life will also hand you the things you want, the things you desire, or seek after; those come, also, with a fight and a kick.

With determination, you can get those things, as well. You must keep taking steps, keep moving. As Lao Tzu said, "The journey of a thousand miles begins with one step."

You will never get anywhere unless you start the journey. A blended family is hard, it is trying, but with one step at a time, you can be successful and win at achieving harmony in your journey.

I spent the last year tying up my life's story to share with you. I overcame losing both parents, burying siblings, enduring miscarriages, being told I would not be a mother, staying persistent until I had my two boys, surviving a devasting divorce, feeling crushed and wounded, feeling a failure and unworthy, knowing grief, and experiencing hopelessness.

I conquered the difficulties of being blended as a family when I could not and did not want to be a stepmother. Looking back,

I consider some of my greatest discoveries along my journey to be these: we all want to feel love and like we belong. I believe family was created to give us fellowship, nurturing, and the sense of belonging. I marvel that no matter the age of my children, I still delight in having conversations with them, spending holidays together, and filling our home with love. We should live with passion, and that includes being enthusiastic about our children, as well as about our spouse.

We are good enough, and we are greater than we think we are. It is likely that you are creating the problems you are trying to solve. If we walk on eggshells around our children or our spouse, it can cause a hostile atmosphere. For one thing, we are not solving anything by walking on eggshells. And second, the others involved do not feel respected or cared for enough to work out the issue. Refuse to live this kind of life.

Relationships are just that – relationships. The good, the bad and the ugly. Relationships are messy. We all long for lasting, fulfilling relationships. They are possible. Imperfect relationships can be turned around when we look inward and see how we are viewing the relationship instead of accusing or blaming the other person. Everyone longs for love, connection, and understanding, especially our children. Not much in life is more fulfilling than being a part of a tribe. A family unit should be the best tribe a child, a husband, a wife, or anyone can experience. That will lead to other tribe experiences with extended family and others to whom we relate. This can open doors to serve others. Passion, growth, depth, and joy are found in good relationships, one of the greatest gifts in life.

I have seen first-hand that all relationships will end, one way or another. I had seven siblings; I have lost six of them that I loved, as well as my parents. I was the baby of the family and so I know that in experiencing loss, we come to realize *all* relationships will end, either by death or by someone's decision to walk away. We must get to a place where it is OK.

My journey has not been easy. Is our family perfect? No. We still have flaws and challenges that we must work through. It is called life. But step by step, we will continue our journey. Still, I have overcome so much! I became a mother. And like Hannah in the Bible, who ultimately would have six children, I also have six children. I am not only a mother to my boys, but also to Chris, Lori, Alijah and Zach. I am a grandmother. I am a conqueror. I am living my best life.

The way through was knowing Jesus made it possible to live life abundantly. Ultimately, we must keep our trust in our Creator, be persistent, keep the faith, stay the course, and let go of past failures. I learned how to get more out of life; to live, laugh, and love with more passion than ever before. After all, we were made on purpose and for a purpose.

I would bet your life's journey has not been easy, either. I hope this inspires you to give yourself grace and to keep striving for improvement. We will never be perfect, but imperfectly perfect will do. This applies not only to us, but to our families and our children. We can leave a legacy for our grandchildren, our great-grandchildren and so on – a legacy of hope, trust, and passion. I hope I inspire you to want to leave a mark in this life, so others can see you were successful in your endeavors. I believe that will empower them to realize they can be successful, too.

The lessons I learned are now being passed on to you. I hope they are valuable, and they help you get more out of life. Know that where you are today is very much based on your past choices. Where you are going tomorrow is very much determined by the choices you make today and, in the days to come as you move forward. Your future and your children's futures depend on you. I want you to live as never before; to take steps, even when you do not understand them, as I did; and to get the life you and your loved ones truly deserve.

MAY'S CUP RUNS OVER

by Ruth Green Pace

May's nest was empty, children, there were none

She prayed to her God and along came a son

First there was one, then there were two

The desires of her heart had finally come true

May rejoiced when her sons were born

She rejoiced in the goodness of the Lord

But her blessings weren't over, they had just begun

God added a daughter, and another son

To Jonathan and Jared, he added Chris and Lori

But it still wasn't the end of the story

Along came Zach, then Alijah

May said, "Lord, I just want to remind you

I ask for one, I ask for two

Now I have six, I think I'm through!

ENDNOTES

1   Wetzel, Jennifer. "A Letter from a Foster Mom." Union City, Tn. June 1, 2022.

2   Selecman, Mattie Jackson. *Lemons on Friday: Trusting God Through My Greatest Heartbreak.* Thomas Nelson, 2021.

3   Natasha Hazlett et al., *Free to Be Me: Breaking Through the Lies to Uncover the True You.* Soul Food Publishing. Franklin, Tn. 2023.

4   Wherry, Montana. "Dear Stepparent" Union City, Tn. July 14, 2022.

ACKNOWLEDGEMENTS

To my sister, Ruth Green Pace, I want to thank you for teaching me so much about our Creator. Your knowledge and your stand throughout your lifetime made a huge impact on me. You are a true servant of God and your dedication to Him and to your calling has inspired so many. I love you.

To Natasha Nassar Hazlett and Rich Hazlett, thank you for being my coaches and mentors in Unstoppable Influence. Without your nudges, and your knowledge of marketing, this book would never have come about. Your insurmountable desire to help others led me in ways I never knew or could have known on my own. You introduced me to several outstanding individuals who inspired me and who coached me. They were guides in training and were present in some of my darkest hours.

Among those individuals:

Don Hutson, best-selling author from Memphis, TN. Don, when you coached me on writing and speaking, I could feel your passion. I grew to love you and your enthusiasm for seeing others grow and share. Thank you for believing in me.

Kristin Oakley, a well-known keynote speaker from Efland, NC. Kristin, you became a forever faithful friend and helped me to get comfortable with speaking. I remember how Facebook was intimidating to me before I met you. Your elegance and your example helped me in so many ways. Thank you.

Coach Val Hylen. You inspired me with your story of how you learned, in a very dire situation, to ask, to believe, to receive, and to trust the process. You laid out life-transforming ways for me to master my mind, move past my fears, and fully trust my Creator.

Cassie Lennox. Thank you for working on the editing of this book and your commitment to helping me get this message out to others. You are a gift to many.

Glenda Caudle. Thank you for the final proof reading and the advice you gave me. You made me feel better knowing that your eyes had been on this book. Your writings at The Union City Daily Messenger were always some of my favorites.

Those holding this book. My prayer is that you receive harmony, peace, and a fulfillment that can only come from God and family. Nothing better can be found than the love of your children.

Above all, I give glory to God Who, despite my ignorance, overlooked and gave me grace, unconditional love, and favor to prevail in this life. The family members, the teams, and the inspiration my Creator led me to are the reason I knew I had to share this story and guide others.

With much love and gratitude to you all,

May

ABOUT THE AUTHOR

 May Simpson is a Certified Personal Empowerment Coach™, with a focus on blended families. She helps families achieve a loving, harmonious environment, so each family member feels loved, respected and free to be themselves. Thriving, not merely surviving, is her mantra!

May knows the challenges that come with a blended family. At the age of 30, she found herself divorced with two small children, ages 3 years and 6 months old. She later remarried. Her second husband, Joe, had two children – 11-year-old twins.

The blended family life is not easy. At one point, May wanted to bail because she felt like she wasn't cut out to be a stepmother. Fortunately, her new husband was determined to make it work. With prayer, counseling and dedication, May and Joe recently celebrated 31 years of marriage.

Along the way, May and Joe adopted two boys, creating a beautiful, yet complex, family made up of stepchildren, biological children, and adopted children.

May feels marriages and families are worth the time and energy it takes to make them work. Some of her greatest joys in life have been because of her blended family. She wants others to experience the same joy and fulfillment that she has.

Through her personal experience and professional training, she has a wealth of tools and knowledge to help families thrive. May is available for speaking engagements, interviews and workshops in addition to her coaching practice.

You can learn more about May at www.HelpFamiliesThrive.com.

Email: May@helpfamiliesthrive.com

Made in the USA
Columbia, SC
13 October 2023

23967331R00115